TERLINGUA
TEACHER

TERLINGUA TEACHER

THE REMARKABLE LESSONS
TAUGHT AND LEARNED
IN A ONE ROOM
TEXAS SCHOOL HOUSE

TRENT JONES

AND

CARLTON STOWERS

IRON MOUNTAIN PRESS

HOUSTON 2009

THIRD PRINTED EDITION 2017

ISBN 0-9745048-3-1
ISBN13: 978-0-9745048-3-4

13   12   11   10   9   8   7   6   5   4

Originally published by Playboy Press in 1978 under the title
WHERE THE RAINBOWS WAIT

Printed and Bound in the United States of America
Front Cover Photo: Courtesy of Shelly Katz

PUBLISHED BY IRON MOUNTAIN PRESS
www.ironmountainpublishing.com

an imprint of

JOHN M. HARDY PUBLISHING COMPANY
www.johnhardypublishing.com

HOUSTON TEXAS

To the students of Terlingua School,
past, present, and future

Olga and Trent Jones, with daughters Anna Maria and Cassandra, in front of the Terlingua post office.
(PHOTO BY SHELLY KATZ)

Prologue

Here, the mantle of God touches you; it is what
Beethoven reached for in music....
— *Ludwig Bemelmans, describing the*
Trans-Pecos region of Texas

Ol' Ludwig must have been boozing it up...
— *H. Allen Smith, commenting*
on Bemelmans's observation

The driver, who had been hired to pull the secondhand mobile home from San Antonio to Terlingua, stepped down from the cab of his truck, shifted his hat to the back of his head, and took a long, sweeping look at the countryside. The new owners of the two-bedroom trailer house had arrived ahead of him and stood on the rock-strewn site, waiting.

Finally the driver approached them, mopped his brow with a red bandanna, and directed his conversation to Trent Jones. "Mister, it ain't none of my business, really, but this country looks like pure hell to me. Dammit, the fact of the matter is, I hate to leave you folks here. You give me the word and I'll turn this rig around and haul that trailer back to San Antonio and not charge you an extra dime."

Trent Jones smiled, looked at his wife and his newborn daughter she was holding. "I guess," he told the driver, "we're here to stay."

"Mister," the driver replied, making no attempt to hide his

concern, "if you aren't crazy now, you damn sure will be in another month or so."

Midway between El Paso and Laredo, the rust-red waters of the Rio Grande follow a southeastern course of mountains and basins before making a great southern bend into the Mexican states of Chihuahua and Coahuila. Located within the bowl of the massive arc is a rugged, remote area known as the Big Bend. Those with a flair for geographic accuracy call it the Trans-Pecos region of Texas.

It is the kind of country only those with the souls of poets or armadillos can appreciate; an endless terrain both barren and beautiful, gentle and hostile, welcoming and forbidding. Within its somewhat vague boundaries is Brewster County, stretching across an area of 5935 square miles, making it larger than several states located on the eastern seaboard of the nation. Brewster County, it can be noted, does not command lukewarm feelings; there are those who are awed by its stark beauty, others who insist that God must have wearied of his task by the time he got around to that part of the world and thus didn't give it his best effort.

It is a country whose montage of mountains, canyons, and desert puzzles and pleases the geologists, beckons the adventurer, and charms the historians, for progress has touched the Trans-Pecos only lightly; many things have gone unchanged since the days when it was still under Spanish and Mexican rule, a part of Chihuahua instead of the Republic of Texas. Perhaps the definitive though unusual description of the area which will serve as the setting for the tome now in your hands was that provided by an old Tex-Mex cowboy, circa 1840, who gave the following directions to a newcomer to the region: "You go south from Fort Davis until you come to the place where the rainbows wait for rain, and the big river is kept in a stone box, and the water runs uphill. And the mountains float in the air, except at night when they go away to play with the other mountains."

He was speaking of the Chisos Mountains which stand sentry over the far-reaching stretches of off-white sand, a range of jagged peaks that violate proper American geographic formality by running east-west instead of north-south. They lend dramatically to the mystery of the area. Chisos is the Spanish word for ghost. The name is appropriate. In the evenings a haze of blues and grays form atop the 7000-foot peaks and lazily floats down into the basins and onto the flatlands, giving the effect of something spiritual, mysterious, and legend-making. At times it appears that the mountaintops are suspended in air, not connected to the earth below. Men have climbed them, never to be heard from again. Stories have it that Mexican general Santa Anna buried great hoards of gold in them and that beasts unknown to modern man roam undetected through their secluded highlands.

It is an area historically populated only by the heartiest of humans and the most withstanding of plant and animal life. Summer temperatures in the canyons and arroyos reach sweat box heights in midday, then drop to a cruel chill at night. It is a land of only two defined seasons: the blistering, energy-draining heat that is summer; and the piercing, sub-freezing, windblown winter in which no amount of clothing is adequate.

In a good year it will rain as much as fourteen inches, most of that coming in swift, violent storms that build up in the West and strike almost without warning, pounding the parched soil and filling the creeks and gullies in a short time. Then the clouds will again disappear, the oppressive sun returns, and steam will rise from the warm sands to create mirages that the most creative of Hollywood directors cannot duplicate.

Generally, vegetation of any type is scarce. One will see an occasional evergreen called a madrona, a scrubby bush-like tree that produces red-yellow berries in early summer; it is referred to by most of the natives as Naked Indian Woman or Lady's Leg. Then there are occasional stands of mesquite, squaw bush, desert willow, huisache, and creosote which dot the seas of sand, the latter a bush that kills any other growth within the immediate radius of where its foul smelling juices drip. Cacti of virtually every variety, shape, and size are easily the front-runner in the botanical competition.

There are bobcats, diamondback rattlers, horned toads, jackrabbits, and occasional mule deer which manage somehow to thrive when mankind with his supposedly superior intellect often doesn't. And the bird-life is an ornithologist's dream come true, the vast region serving as a home for a variety of owls, hawks, finches, and warblers.

The Trans-Pecos stands apart from all other parts of Texas. In a state where they play big league baseball indoors, where people have oil wells pumping at three, sometimes four, depths, and where stores publish elaborate Christmas catalogues ballyhooing

His and Her private airplanes, the Trans-Pecos remains a region where life and living are as rugged as any Old West drama ever staged. It is a part of the world where residents stand hospitably ready to offer guests a beer or something with a bit more bite, yet dread a request for nothing more than a glass of ice water — for both ice and water are selfishly guarded luxuries.

It was in this part of the world that I chose to teach, in a small one-room schoolhouse that was a throwback to frontier times. But I wanted challenges — and I certainly got them here....

Five years ago I was earning $9000 a year teaching special education classes to San Antonio fourth-graders. My peers and students alike had nominated me as one of the nation's Outstanding Elementary Teachers. I lived with my wife and infant daughter in a comfortable home in a fashionable residential section of town. By measure of most yardsticks applied within our society, I was a young man of no small success.

On the other hand, I had freeways to maneuver each morning and the same battle to fight on the way home every evening. There was the mortgage, the bureaucratic leanings of a big-city school board, and the constant high-speed dash of friends and neighbors running everywhere and, so far as I was able to see, getting nowhere. By my own yardstick, I was falling woefully short of my own definition of success.

I wanted out of the rat race. My father is a retired Corpus Christi criminal lawyer, and there was a time when I aspired to follow in his footsteps. Instead, I gave up my pre-law courses early at Trinity University and earned a bachelor's degree in speech and drama. I just felt I would be happier teaching, working with kids. I felt I could make some kind of contribution. I'm not sure Dad understands it to this day.

Following graduation, my first teaching job was with the South San Antonio Independent School District where I had two jobs at once: teaching special education classes for slow learners throughout the system and also taking daily lessons to the homebound students of all black Booker T. Washington Elementary. I enjoyed the teaching, but at the same time I became more and more frustrated with my situation. I was responsible for a large number of kids and I couldn't spend as much time with each individual as I wanted to, especially since it seemed like I spent half my time going to teachers' meetings and seminars. My frustration grew to the point where I was seriously concerned that it would affect my teaching. I decided it was time to look elsewhere, and my wife, Olga, agreed.

We had done quite a bit of traveling out into the Big Bend country and we had really fallen in love with the area. We'd even bought a little forty acre plot and used to talk a lot about maybe one day living on it. Olga thought it was one of those wild kinds of things you dream about and talk about but never really expect will come true.

Then we heard about a small one room schoolhouse in the ghost town of Terlingua. There, on the southern edge of Brewster County, at the base of the Christmas Mountains, stood the Terlingua Common School, serving as an academic oasis for the sons and daughters of the 100 or so adults who resided within the far reaching boundaries of the school district. The multiple job of principal/teacher/ janitor had come open, offering an annual salary of $4500 for carrying out the duties of principal/teacher with an additional $50 per month for janitorial work.

Once a thriving center of quicksilver mining, the town now was nothing more than scattered adobe remains of another time in Texas history. Only once a year, when an oddball assortment of chili fanciers, celebrities, and curiosity seekers gathered for the highly publicized World's Championship Chili Cook-Off, did it merit being referred to as anything but the ghost town it officially is. Yet because a few people still lived in the area, there was a post office and a one room school where children from grades one to eight wrestled with the thundering mysteries of reading, writing, and arithmetic.

Never mind that the salary would make it economically impossible to enjoy such conveniences as a telephone. So what if I had to haul water five miles to fill the 1800-gallon tank which would sit behind the trailer house purchased with the remainder of our savings. Terlingua, with its quiet, its solitude, and its exciting challenge, was what I was looking for.

I applied.

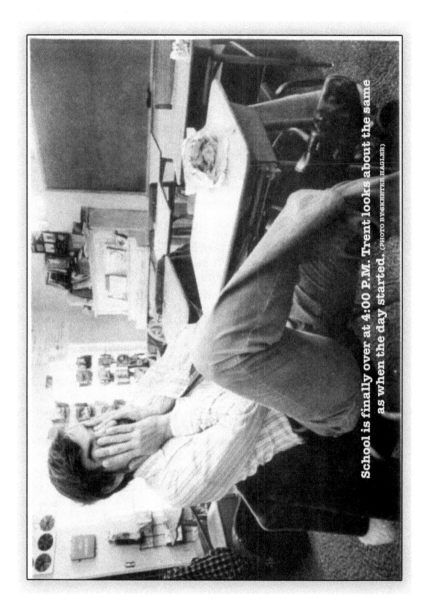

School is finally over at 4:00 P.M. Trent looks about the same as when the day started. (PHOTO BY SKRFTER HAGLER)

I

❧ ❧ ❧

The plumbing at the school was again out of order. Faced with no other alternative, I sent those students needing to be excused "over the hill." For the girls it was a considerable imposition. But the boys didn't seem to mind. "You know, Mr. Jones," one said as he returned to the classroom, "I bet the Terlingua School is the only one in the world with a five-thousand-acre bathroom."

Olga stood, shading her eyes against the midday August sun, laughing at the absurdity of it all. At the same time I was doing my dead level best to ignore her, hoping all the while that no one would pick that particular time to stop by and find me standing on top of the house conducting what my amused wife had come to call The Great Experiment. I had already gained a reputation in the community as something of a spit-and-a-prayer handyman and now here I was, naked to the waist, covered with sticky tar which I hadn't the foggiest idea how I was going to get off, pouring buckets of water onto the roof whose temperature at that moment must have been at least 150 degrees.

As I would pour, the steam would rise from the hot tin and tarpaper, prompting another round of laughter from below. I said nothing; just lowered the bucket to the ground by rope so it could be refilled. Frankly, I was hard pressed to see even the most remote humor in the situation until Anna, our eldest daughter, walked out into the yard, a frown fixed on her face, and approached her mother.

"Mommy," she said, "would you please ask daddy to quit making it rain while I'm trying to use the bathroom?"

Her request duly presented, she turned and marched back into the house. I looked down at Olga and began to laugh myself.

A sense of humor, as you will find, is one of the necessary tools of survival for those who choose to set up house keeping in the middle of the desert.

There was, understand, method to my madness. We had recently moved from the trailer in which we had lived for the first three years of our residence in Terlingua and were now in the final stages of converting the old, now abandoned school into our new home. Earlier in the summer our new adobe school building had been completed on the school grounds, and since there were no plans for use of the old building, I had approached the school board about living in it. They had agreed, and suddenly we felt as if we were moving into town except for the fact that out here we have no real town to move into.

In addition to providing us with more room, the new home-site offered the convenience of running water and the fact that I would only be roughly fifty feet from work instead of the ten miles it had been when we lived up the highway in our little trailer. And while its architect no doubt never intended the building to be used as a home for a family of four, we had, with a partition here, a wall there, and a couple of additional windows, converted it into a very comfortable house. Olga had put up curtains, placed her house plants all around, and arranged the furniture so artistically that I suggested she take pictures and drop them in the mail to *House Beautiful* or someone. Ernie Harmon, a retired carpet layer who had recently moved to Terlingua with hopes of establishing a Baptist mission, had helped me lay linoleum in the kitchen area and build Olga some additional shelving. All in all, after our weeks of work, the place had quietly taken on the warmth a home is supposed to have.

However, I had saved the most challenging chore for last. It was necessary to enlarge the bathroom, installing a shower, rerouting pipes, and putting up more shelving. The job, which I had liberally figured would require two days, was only completed after a week and a half. All that remained now, though, was for me to dab a little tar here and there on the new roof I had put over the remodeled bathroom to make sure there would be no leaks when it rained.

"You had better get right on it," Olga had said. "It could rain any month now."

That remark, an obvious reference to the fact that this part of the world gets only slightly more rainfall than the Mojave Desert, came after I had carefully outlined my testing plan to her. What I would do, I explained, was take a bucket of tar up on the roof with me, then hang a rope down to which she could tie the handle of a bucket of water. I would hoist the water up and pour some over a small area of the roof, she could go inside and see where the leaks were, and I would then patch them with the tar. I hadn't, I told her, gone to college for nothing.

After an hour, several gallons of tar, and enough buckets

of water to make my back feel as if I'd been breaking horses all day, the holes were all patched, the project complete. And with little time to spare. I had already posted notice down at Daisy Adams's post office that school registration would be held the following week.

That night we put the children to bed and sat outside in the cooled night air. Relaxed by the kind of tiredness that accompanies a feeling of accomplishment, I sat listening to Olga play her guitar and watching as the moon began to climb over the mountains. We were both feeling quite good about our new location, neither of us having ever thought a trailer a proper home — particularly after the first few times we had to anchor it down to keep seventy mile-per-hour winds from blowing it off its foundation and down into a gully that ran behind it. The old schoolhouse was going to do nicely.

As we talked, the rising moon erased some of the darkness and I could clearly see the new school across the way. It had been built with $12,000 of revenue sharing money donated to the school by Brewster County. While not much larger than the previous one, it would be more comfortable. The kids, I was sure, would be pleased with it.

"By the way," I said after Olga had finished a song she had been practicing for some time, "one of my ex-students came by the other day. You remember Kenneth Davis, the boy we had the first year we were here whom I had so much trouble with about chewing tobacco in class?"

The smile on her face made it obvious that she remembered

the youngster who had since moved away.

"What did he have to say?"

"Oh, he said he heard I was still here, so he had to come by and see for himself before he would believe it. He told me it must be a miracle or something since the kids had always managed to run the teacher off about every other year when he was here."

"Maybe you were lucky he graduated after your first year," Olga suggested.

"You know what else he said? He said he knew he had been a big pain in the ass to me but that he thought I was the best teacher this school has ever had. He said he actually felt he had learned some things that last year. That made me feel really good. I thought it was nice of him to stop by and tell me that."

"Was he still chewing tobacco?"

"Biggest wad you ever saw, but he didn't spit on the floor this time."

"Well," Olga said as she rose to go inside, "maybe you managed to teach him something after all. Let's go to bed."

We spent most of that first night learning that there were bugs — quite literally — to be ironed out before our new house would be comfortable. For most of the night Olga was up swatting mosquitoes and using one of her slippers to kill various intruding spiders and scorpions. Every time things would get quiet and sleep seemed a real possibility, one of the mousetraps we had set would snap, signaling a quick death for yet another unwanted visitor.

Then, in the early morning hours, a hard northern wind came

up to make me aware of several drafts coming through the wall behind our bed. In my bleary state, in fact, I discovered a gaping hole between the wall and the roof which provided us with more air conditioning than we felt need for. Finally we moved the bed to the center of the room, I stuffed a pair of my pajamas into the crack in the wall, and turned out the lights.

"Welcome to your new home, honey," I said to Olga. She did not answer. The covers were pulled over her head.

The second year I taught here only three students came to the school on registration day. I had more than a few anxious moments during the days between registration and the first official day of school, certain that if a considerably larger number of students didn't show up my idyllic dream of making a career of being a one room schoolteacher would go down the drain after just one year. Gradually, though, more students straggled in until the enrollment grew to eleven, then twelve pupils. It was an ideal number for one teacher to work with.

In the years that followed I learned not to become too concerned over the poor attendance on registration day and in fact considered doing away with it altogether, simply waiting to register the children on the first day of school. Each year most of the students would show up that first day, all freshly scrubbed, carrying their lunches, and radiating their marvelous mixture of excitement and anxiety. For three years the enrollment had always leveled off at somewhere between ten and fifteen. It was as near perfect as I could have wished for it to be.

So, when twenty-six students arrived, ready to begin classes this year, I was flabbergasted. Not only was there a larger than usual group back from the previous year, which of course I'd expected, but the classroom was dotted with new faces. Obviously Terlingua was booming, so much so that I had to leave Olga to pass out the registration forms and check out books while I took the pickup and drove up to see Glenn Pepper, president of our school board, to get some extra desks we stored in one of his sheds.

"How's business?" Pepper asked as I arrived.

"I've got kids hanging from the rafters down there," I said.

Pepper made the observation that the salesmen who had been hired to promote real estate deals for the nearby Terlingua Ranch must have all been devoted family men. If he was trying to make a joke, I didn't have time at the moment to laugh.

The first day of classes in our brand new school building, then, made several things abundantly clear. Our prize new structure — complete with carpeting that had been donated to us by an Alpine apartment complex owner who was remodeling and about to throw it away — was already too small. We had been sure that it would see us through the possibility of any gradual enrollment growth for years to come, but right at the start it was overcrowded.

It was also obvious that the teacher was going to have to spread himself more thinly than he had been doing in years past. Fifteen minutes of individual instruction would have to be whittled down to five, maybe less. I would also have to call Alpine and set up delivery of additional textbooks as soon as possible.

What had already promised to be a busy year suddenly loomed as the most challenging of my teaching career. The number of students and the crowded schoolroom were just part of the task to be dealt with over the next nine months. Additionally, there was the matter of meeting a long list of standards set down by the Texas Education Agency's accreditation board if the Terlingua School was to survive past the term we were preparing to begin.

And, as usual, the water lines were acting up.

I can well remember my first experience with the troublesome water lines that serve the school. I was new, trying very hard to make a favorable impression on the students, and one morning one of the girls went to use the bathroom and returned to report that there was no water pressure. I investigated the situation and discovered a leak out on the school grounds. Water was going everywhere, thus there was nothing to do but call a halt to class and try to attend to the immediate problem. I told the kids to come outside and I would show them how to fix a leaking water line.

I got a shovel, a screwdriver, and a pipe clamp from my truck and began my impromptu instruction on water line repair. As the students watched silently, I dug up the line and then got down on my hands and knees to try and put the clamp over the break. I was getting wet and muddy. The children remained silent. After several minutes it was obvious to me that I was failing mightily and I began to try desperately to think of some graceful way to save face.

In the meantime one of the older students had quietly disappeared behind the school building and returned with a long strip of rubber he had cut from an old inner tube. "Mr. Jones," he said, "if you'll get up, I'll fix that for you."

By that time I was ready to accept help from anybody so I got up and he quickly knelt down, careful not to get himself dirty, and wrapped the pipe with the rubber strip, pulled it tight, tied it off neatly, and rose. The leak had been stopped.

I smiled sheepishly, thanked him, and quickly excused myself to the again functional bathroom to try and clean some of the mud off before I resumed class.

Since that day I have held a deep appreciation for old inner tubes. If all the strips of rubber I've tied to rusting, cracking pipes were tied end-to-end, they would likely reach from here to the Mexican border. Repairing the water lines, I would come to learn, was as much a part of the duties of the Terlingua teacher as lesson plans.

Olga and I had, in fact, encountered water problems from the moment we arrived. For the first few months we lived here, we had precious little water except that which I hauled daily from the school in a couple of rusty fifty gallon barrels. I would back the pickup up to two other barrels I had mounted on an old trailer bed and used a small electric water cooler pump to get the water from one set of barrels to the other. It was as jury-rigged a setup as you will ever see; didn't always work; and when it did, transferred the water at the blazing rate of about a gallon every five minutes. It was a long tedious process every day.

We would then take the water into the house in buckets as we needed it — which was often since Anna was still in diapers at the time. Water for bathing had to be heated on the stove, and the toilet had to be filled by hand each time after it was flushed. I would quickly learn that it takes an amazing three gallons of water just to flush a toilet once. It seemed like every spare minute I had was spent trying to see that we had water available — which often prompted me to use the English language in a manner hardly becoming a schoolteacher, I'm afraid.

A lot of the problems we originally experienced would not have come up had it not been for the stubbornness of a local restaurant owner and school board member named Ray Potts. For some reason he and I never managed to hit it off. I later learned, in fact, that he had been the only member of the board against hiring me in the first place.

At any rate, we had arrived in Terlingua with our trailer, assuming that we would be allowed to park it on the school grounds. We tried to get in touch with Jim Blanton, the board member I had been corresponding with, but found out he and his family were out of town — they worked in the summers as a country music band, playing at a place in Durango, Colorado, until school started each year. So I went to see Ray Potts at his restaurant. Suffice it to say he did not bother to roll out any red carpet. We talked for a minute or two and then I asked him if it would be okay to park the trailer on the far side of the school grounds.

A man of few words, he said, "Hell, no."

I literally begged him to reconsider. I told him there was no electricity or water or even a septic tank on the piece of property we owned. I pointed out that we had a small baby. He just smiled one of those kinds of smiles that make you want to knock somebody's teeth out and said, "Well, I suppose maybe you shoulda thought about some of those things before you decided to move out here. The fact of the matter is, everybody out here suffers in some way or another. I can't say I can see any reason why you folks should be different." End of conversation.

Fortunately Ray Potts was not the best example of Terlingua's citizenry. After we had hauled our trailer the additional ten miles down the road and parked it on the acreage we had bought several years earlier during our vacationing trips out here, several people came by to lend a hand at getting us settled.

One was Emerald Martin who lived about a mile on down the road. Hearing of our problem, he offered to pipe water to us from his place for $20 a month. Our problem, then, was solved — until Potts got word of the plan. He immediately went to Emerald and pointed out that he owned a strip of land between our properties and had no intention of allowing pipes to be laid across it. My hopes of getting water and my opinion of Ray Potts reached simultaneous new lows.

One of the great ironies of Potts's hardheadedness came a few days later when, after thinking over the proposition Emerald had made to me, he went to my neighbor and asked Emerald what he would charge to pipe water onto Potts's own land. Emerald, a man with a good grasp of how to deal with people like Potts, suggested that the restaurant owner perform an unnatural act on himself, then ordered him off his land.

It did absolutely nothing to solve my dilemma, but the personal satisfaction felt so good I had pangs of guilt.

Eventually it was my parents who came to the rescue. A couple of months after we settled in Terlingua they came out for a visit. Both made a brave effort to accept what we were doing, though I think Mother would dearly have loved to go off somewhere and have a good cry, and Dad probably wished I'd seek some professional help from one of his psychiatrist friends. With a son who is an assistant district attorney, another in the state legislature, and a daughter in college anxiously looking forward to the day she'll be able to join a dance company, my parents made no pretense of completely understanding my choice.

Instead, however, they suggested that we take a drive over to Alpine. While there, Dad bought us an 1800-gallon water tank and some pumps. At the same time mother was off buying a heater to keep us from "freezing to death" in the winter.

If I have ever received a more welcome gift than that water tank and pumps, it slips my mind at the moment. Furthermore, no sooner had I set it up than Glenn Pepper and his wife came by and offered to loan us a 250-gallon tank I could mount on a trailer for hauling water to our new tank. Life was suddenly becoming easier.

Which isn't to say it was like living on a lake front lot. With the new equipment came new problems. It seemed the pumps, though new, were in constant need of repair. Since the ground on which our trailer sat was almost solid rock, it was impossible to dig trenches to bury pipes. So as soon as winter set in, the pipes froze and burst. The pumps did likewise and all the water drained from the tank, leaving us a front yard you could have played hockey on until the sun melted the ice away. I was back to a steady routine of replacing and repairing.

The arrival of summer didn't lessen the problems. The days would get so hot, sometimes to 112 degrees, that the pipes would swell and burst, and there'd go all the water again. And one afternoon, the makeshift trailer I used to haul water on blew a tire, came loose from the truck, and went toppling down the hill behind our house. I finally managed to get it back up and rewelded, rebolted, wired, and generally patched back together the best way I could.

After our first couple of months in Terlingua I felt more in need of a vacation than I ever had in my life. If we had been able to afford a telephone, I just might have called that driver and taken him up on his offer to haul us back to San Antonio.

The water situation at the school wasn't much better. Prior to this year we never had water more than fifty percent of the time, and during those times we did have it the pressure was so low that it would take at least ten minutes for the toilet to refill. The pipes were in such constant need of repair that it became almost routine for me to spend my lunch hour patching leaks.

Five residences and the Study Butte Cafe were served by the same water line we used and it seemed everyone held the other responsible for maintenance of the system. Consequently, if I wanted water at the school, I had to do the repair work. By the time school was out last year the water line was more like a sprinkler system, and the last few weeks of classes were conducted without benefit of any water at all. The students brought their own drinking water and kept it beside their desks and had to resort to nature's great outdoors instead of the bathroom. I silently prayed that the public health inspector wouldn't stop by for one of his infrequent inspections before school was out. If he had, classes at the Terlingua School would no doubt have been adjourned a couple of weeks early.

I complained to the school board at every opportunity, and they finally assured me they would see to the problem during the summer. By the time school opened this fall, I was assured, water would at long last not be a distracting problem.

I have learned, however, that if something needs to be done it takes more than simply asking and waiting for the work to begin. Two weeks before school was to begin, we still had no water line. I went to the school board again to see what progress was being made. They had already reluctantly agreed to hire a professional pump company in Alpine to install a new line which would be the sole property of the school, but immediately began explaining to me the numerous problems that stood between them and completion of the task. Our proposed new water line would have to cross the highway, it was pointed out, and that would involve obtaining permission from the state highway department. A lot of paper work would be involved. Then it requires a special machine to drill a hole under a highway and, word has it, there are only a couple of them in the state. No telling when we could get one of them down here. That, I was told, was the holdup.

"We're never going to get that water line," Olga said that evening when I told her the situation. "Nobody has even made an effort to get the work under way."

The following morning I drove to El Paso to visit one of the highway department's central offices to find out for myself what needed to be done. In twenty minutes I had explained our problem, filled out a few papers, and was on my way to visit Henderson Pump Company in Alpine. The foreman was quite amused when I asked about the special machine necessary to drill under a highway.

"You tell your school board people to call me and give me the word that they want me to do the job and we'll be down there just as soon as we can," he told me.

Using a handmade tool operated by two men, the hole was drilled under the highway in eight hours, at a cost of $200. We would have to tolerate the on-again, off-again water system for the first few weeks of school, but in a short time the Terlingua School would have a water system that actually worked. I felt we were moving right along into the twentieth century.

Despite the large number of students, things quickly settled into a workable routine. Of course the excitement of being in a new building was evident, and the kids gave Olga and me no rest until they got a grand tour, en masse, of the old school that we had converted into our living quarters. They were amazed at the new look the place had taken on. Second grader Bubba Staton, my budding artist, said it looked like a mansion to him and he was going right back to his desk and draw a picture of it. I told him he would have to make a quick job of it because the last period of school that day had been set aside for his sister Kim's birthday party. (Since most people are so far removed from one another out here, we have made a tradition of allowing the students to have their birthday parties at school so all their friends can attend.)

Kim's mother brought punch and cookies and we played a few games and presents were opened. As the children were leaving, Kim came over, hugged my neck, and said, "Thank you for a fun party, I'm the first one to have a birthday in the new school!"

There have been more days than I would like to remember when I felt things didn't go too well academically at the Terlingua School, but I don't believe we've ever had a bad birthday party.

II

襟 襟 襟

Frontier life was harsh for the young schoolmistress, conditions
were primitive, and the financial rewards were small. Jeanette
Dow Stephens taught school at Terlingua during the 1909-1910
school year, received $65 per month, and held classes in a large
old tenthouse with long bench- like seats.
— From Quick-Silver: Terlingua and the Chisos Mining Company *by Kenneth Baxter Ragsdale*

Well, at least we got out of the tent.
— Trent Jones

It's strange how different a place looks when you attach a
permanence to it; when it becomes your place of daily residence
rather than an occasionally visited vacation spot.

For several years, during spring breaks and summer vaca-
tions, Olga and I had traveled to this part of the country,
delighting in the charm and quiet beauty of its open spaces, its
barren landscape, and the hardscrabble simplicity of the life-
style. Terlingua, with its Chevron Service Station, its cafe with
unmatched silverware, cold beer, and vinyl stools, its seldom used
tourist court and trailer park, struck us as something straight
out of a Wild West fairy tale. We romanticized it unmercifully to
our friends back home who had never been there and we spent a
great deal of time between return trips discussing the possibility
of making it our home.

To the casual visitor escaping for a day from the bindings of
the city, Terlingua's slow paced way of life was magnetic. There

was no clamor of traffic, no harassed looking businessmen rushing to grab a sandwich on their lunch hour, no throngs of shoppers. For one seeking the avenue by which to travel back to the basics and away from the chrome and glass world which seemed to have been chasing its own tail through most of the last twenty years, Terlingua represented something of a wayside Shangri-la.

Each visit would find us giving closer inspection to the town — if you can call a half-dozen frame and adobe buildings a town. We came to notice even the slightest change in the landscape from trip to trip: any new trailer house that might be anchored in place; the barren spot left by some family we had not even come to know. We watched for new signs of ownership and occasionally visited the post office operated by a charming and talkative woman named Daisy Adams, not anticipating mail, of course, but to hear her tell of the region's colorful history.

We looked, we listened, and we longed to retreat into this world and become a part of it; to experience the challenge and adventure that passes the city dweller by.

I only wish we had checked to see if the place had a laundromat.

Looking back to those days of dreaming about hauling a trailer of our own to Terlingua, I would have to say that sound judgment could have been better exercised had we taken time to look beyond the stark beauty of the region and its beckoning peace and quiet and inspiring sunsets and learned what people living there did when dirty diapers got knee-deep. Or what number they dialed when in need of a doctor. Or how they figured on learning if we had collided with another planet since there was no television reception and the radio broadcasts came only late at night when the border stations fill the airways with their 50,000-watt mail order religion and jingly gospel singing.

The fact is, a city boy pioneer's romantic dreams are often accompanied by sizable blind spots. Preventive maintenance, for example, was a notion that was foreign to me; I grew up following the credo passed on to me by my lawyer father — problems are best dealt with only when and if they occur.

In the early days of our Terlingua residence, they occurred in bunches, sometimes overlapping, intermingling, and breeding spin-off problems. Try, for instance, to teach a group of children that fully three-fourths of the earth's surface is covered by water while at the same time explaining to them that there isn't enough of it immediately at hand to allow the flushing of the school toilet.

But one adapts to the day-to-day tribulations. As time passed, it became as natural to tell the children going out for recess to watch carefully for rattlesnakes as it had been to warn the kids back in San Antonio to look out for cars. As you become a part of the country you learn to tolerate the weather and the constant water problem. After a while you find that seeing the "Mary Tyler Moore Show" each week isn't really all that necessary to man's survival, and you learn, too, that simply because a community is small it is not spared its ration of soreheads, political backbiters, and those bent on dealing out social injustices.

All in all I can think of very few crises we have experienced since coming to Terlingua that we weren't able to look back on and laugh about once given the benefit of time and hindsight. One of the exceptions, however, was the problem that faced the school as the 1976-77 academic year began.

The Terlingua School has not always been in the location it now occupies. Time was, in fact, when it was a large four room stucco building in Terlingua proper, surrounded by the adobe homes of mine workers, a company store, a jail, and the various other business establishments one generally expected to find in a turn-of-the-century boom town.

Until 1942, when the Chisos Mining Company finally closed down, Terlingua owned the widespread reputation of being the country's largest producer of cinnabar, from which quicksilver — or mercury — is extracted. The boom had begun in earnest in 1903 with the first recorded recovery of the valuable ore from the desert mountainsides and would, under the dictating eye of a Cleveland, Ohio, native named Howard Perry, make Chisos one of the most lucrative mining operations in the nation despite the obscurity of its geographic location. Perry, a short, gruff man who had once moved comfortably in eastern social circles, is said to have gained control of the land when a debtor had been unable to repay a small loan. Upon having his new holdings surveyed, he learned that the cinnabar was waiting to be mined.

Once aware that a huge fortune awaited him in this remote part of the country, Perry took leave of his yachting and formal dinner parties to come to Texas and play the role of pioneer businessman. And as his riches grew, so did Terlingua. Once nothing more than a way station trading post, it exploded into a full-blown frontier town — with everything owned and run by Perry.

He saw to it, the stories go, that a profit was turned at every opportunity. The men who worked the mines, for instance, were paid at the end of each day's work and would then proceed to the company store where they would return their hard-earned silver dollars for groceries and staples for themselves and their families. If there was anything left over, it was usually spent at the Perry-owned saloon. Thus, by the time the miners fell into bed at night, almost all the money they had earned was back in Perry's hands.

While it is generally reported that Perry had precious little compassion for those whose back-breaking labor was essential to his quest for wealth, he did see to it that the community had such first-time conveniences as a weekly mail delivery from Alpine, a resident doctor, and a quality school for which he hired as many as four teachers to educate as many as 150 children of miners in a single school term. Naturally, it was called the Perry School. Perry had assumed, and rightfully so, that the promise of a first-rate education would lure all the workers he would need to his isolated empire. Teachers, hired and paid by Perry, were not, however, provided undue privileges; they paid Perry rent for the adobe homes they occupied while living in Terlingua.

Meanwhile, Perry built himself a proud Spanish-style mansion on the mountainside overlooking the town and the mines, hiring an entourage of servants to attend his every want. When the house was in order, he dispatched a train to bring his wife from Chicago to live with him in the desolate Texas mining town. Historians say she spent but one night in the mansion, not even bothering to unpack her bags, before returning to Chicago. A disappointed Perry saw her off on the train at Alpine and returned to his newfound holdings. Alone in the massive, echoing house, he would spend evenings sitting in a cane-bottom rocking chair on the porch, looking out at the majestic sunsets and star-filled nights of the Trans-Pecos. At the first hint of daylight he was at the mines, overseeing the work that was making him a richer man by the day.

With the demise of the mines came the equally swift demise of Terlingua. Still, those who stubbornly remained continued to see the need for education for their children and managed to maintain a school of sorts at various locations throughout the area. Sometimes school was held in the kitchens of various ranch houses, once in nearby Lajitas, and in Study Butte — wherever there was a large enough concentration of youngsters and someone willing to assume the responsibility of teaching them.

More than once I have walked among the ruins of old Terlingua, stopping to look at the shell remains of the old Perry School and trying to imagine how education was back then. It was, I'm sure, no easy task to teach under the conditions laid down by Mr. Perry. No doubt the list of hardships encountered by the various teachers summoned to Terlingua would make my own tribulations seem like so much nitpicking.

I can only wonder, though, what the tyrannical Mr. Perry and his hapless teachers would have done had they been faced with the chore of dealing with an organization known as the Texas Education Agency Accreditation Board.

While those who remained after the mines closed viewed school as a social necessity, they soon realized it was also a financial liability, and therefore it operated on a budget that was but a short step away from being nonexistent. Volunteer teachers were called to duty whenever they could be found, and if the need arose for supplies or repairs of any of the various structures the students occupied over ensuing years, the locals simply pitched in and saw to it that the money was raised. Secure in its isolation, the Terlingua School lived by its own rules, governed to a large degree by the handful of residents who had children of school age.

Things began to change about ten years ago when a Texas real-estate development company known as the Terremar Corporation purchased one of the largest ranches in the area and launched an enthusiastic advertising campaign to sell people small tracts of land at what seemed unbelievably low prices. City people who dreamed of escape to the hinterland readily bought the ten, twenty, and forty acre plots for small down payments and modest monthly installments. The American Dream, it seemed, was suddenly coming to life in the Trans-Pecos of Texas. New people came, slowly at first and then in a rush. Some pulled mobile homes behind them; some came in campers. A few built cabins, others brought only tents. It was like a miniature land rush, as each hurried to the Terlingua area to stake his claim. With the rush of new people, strangers to the region, came unrest and ultimate upheaval. Many of the longtime ranchers, men who had inherited their land from their fathers, who had inherited it from fathers before them, grew disillusioned with the sudden changes in their world. Too many new people, carving up the land with a maze of roads leading to their places in the sun, bringing their city ways with them, created an atmosphere in which many of the old ranchers could no longer survive. They, too, eventually sold to realtors or wealthy Dallas and Houston doctors and lawyers in search of camping and hunting hideaways and themselves moved away. Thus, in a short period of time a new group of people had claimed the area. The Trent Joneses were among them.

As this transition was being made, sweeping changes were also taking place within the academic community of Texas. With new and aggressive attention being focused on education, more and more taxes were being collected to match state funds for new and inventive programs. The smaller, financially pressed school districts were the first to feel the sting of the broadening educational demands.

Terlingua, in the finest of pioneering traditions, fought the progress tooth and nail, kicking, screaming, and vowing, by God, to continue to do things its way. That such stubbornness was going to be put to a supreme test, however, became evident the day that House Bill 1126, a public school finance plan passed by the state legislature, arrived in my mail in the spring of 1975.

In essence the bill demanded that all Texas schools, regardless of size or location, maintain progressive standards consistent with those set down by the state rather than simply abiding by those of local school districts which chose to keep the tax rate low in order to stay in business. What it meant was that the Terlingua School would finally have to fall into step with the other schools throughout Texas. It also meant that in order to comply with the Texas Education Code we would have to become fully accredited or face consolidation with the Alpine Independent School District. Simply stated, a great number of improvements would have to be made within a two-year time period or Terlingua would find itself without a school.

While the notification presented a list of demanding challenges, I enthusiastically viewed it as the salvation of our school. Certainly the school board and members of the community would realize the tremendous amount of work that needed to be done and attack the problem with great vigor. The prospect of being absorbed by the Alpine school district, eighty miles down the highway, would no doubt serve as enough of a motivating factor to call up a full-scale community effort to save the school. After all, what parent would want their child bussed 160 miles round-trip each day to attend school?

I immediately went to the school board with the list of things that would have to be done. First, the land in the school district would have to be reevaluated so that action could be taken to raise taxes for the next year. A book of school policies, detailing the overall operation of the school, would have to be written. School board policies would have to be set in writing. A curriculum guide, detailing the teaching procedures of each subject at each grade level, would have to be prepared. Additional storage space would have to be made available. A better library with new encyclopedias and an improved list of books would have to be arranged. Standardized tests would have to be given the students on a regular basis to assess the values and progress of our educational program.... The list seemed to go on and on.

Joe Fandrich, president of the school board at the time, looked over the list, frowned, and said, "Those people in Austin are never satisfied unless they're meddling in somebody's business. They've got no idea what it's like out here. This isn't Dallas or Houston — hell, we're just a little bitty ol' school trying to keep the doors open. This whole thing is totally unrealistic."

"Unrealistic or not, Joe," I said, "we've got to follow it to the letter or they're going to shut us down just as sure as I'm standing here."

"I wouldn't be too sure about that," he replied.

"Well, they're sending out a detailed book of requirements for accreditation," I explained, "and as soon as it gets here I think the school board ought to meet and talk over how to get started."

He nodded in agreement but without the degree of enthusiasm or concern I had anticipated. "Don't you worry about it," he said, "we'll take care of everything."

I was convinced that he had not grasped the magnitude of the problem.

Joe Fandrich, a stocky man in his mid-thirties who wears a full, reddish beard with great pride, had been appointed to the Terlingua school board shortly after I was hired. A geologist, he had developed a local fluorspar mine which prospered, making him one of the most successful people in the area.

When I first met him I was delighted that he was a member of the school board. A native of Colorado, he was a college graduate, something of an intellectual, and a strong willed man who got things done. It was Joe who saw to it that the first telephone was installed at the school and that a fire extinguisher was purchased. When I pointed out that one electrical outlet at the school wasn't adequate, he quickly saw to it that wiring and an additional outlet were installed. His wife had taught at the school a few years prior to my arrival, and I assumed that her knowledge of its operations and its day-to-day problems had been imparted to him, thus placing him in a position to better understand my occasional requests.

Slowly, however, it became obvious to me that Joe was not altogether happy with some of my methods of operation. At the time I was hired, no one had given me any instructions on what to do and not do, what policies to follow, or what kind of chain of command to be aware of. Only gradually was it becoming clear to me that Joe felt the need to fully exercise his role of school board president. Finally, he made it clear that I was to seek his permission before engaging in any projects relative to the school.

It wasn't an easy demand to meet in view of the fact he lived fifteen miles away, over some of the worst dirt roads in the area. More times than not I would make the drive out there only to find him not at home. He seemed, in fact, never to be around when I would make the rounds of the school board members to get them to sign my paycheck which was sent unsigned to me by County Judge Sam Thomas each month.

By the end of that first year, an uncomfortable feeling would come over me every time I had to confront Joe Fandrich on a school matter. It would not get better in days to come.

When the manual from the state board of education arrived, however, I dutifully drove out to his house to give it to him and again try to make him aware of the need to begin work on the problem immediately.

"I called Austin the other day," I told him, "and they told me that there are several things on the list that we should have been working on as early as a year ago."

He took the book from me and said he would look it over. As I drove back toward home, bouncing along the potted, rock-strewn road, I felt a rushing wave of concern. Originally it had seemed to me that the basic problem would simply be meeting all the necessary requirements in the time allotted. Now, I feared, convincing people of the problem itself was going to be an equally hard task.

Before going home I stopped by Ron Willard's service station to advise him of the arrival of the manual and then went by Villa de la Mina to tell Glenn Pepper. As the other two members of the school board, they had not been nearly so active as Fandrich, content to show up at the irregular school board meetings. I made an appeal to each of them to immediately look into the situation and take an active role in seeking resolution to the problem.

Back home, I told Olga of the arrival of the much awaited book and that I had taken it out to Joe.

"What did he have to say?" she asked.

After I related our brief conversation, she shook her head. "If you have any little chores around the house you've been wanting to do, I suggest you get them done pretty soon," she said.

"Why's that?" I asked.

"Because pretty soon, after Joe Fandrich has mulled over this accreditation situation enough for him to get it through his thick, arrogant head that it really is going to have to be taken care of, I've got a pretty good idea who's going to be doing all the work."

I did too.

There was yet another matter included in the state board of education's demands: House Bill 1126 gave teachers statewide raises and noted that state funds would be immediately cut off to any school district that did not comply.

Thus as the time approached for the final school board meeting of the year, I included the new salary figure when, as usual, I filled out my contract for the following academic year, and presented it to the board for their signatures. In my delight at the prospect of additional income, however, I had failed to consider the reaction of the school officials.

Fandrich was the first to question the new salary figure. Even when shown the figures set down by the state board, he balked, making no move toward signing it as the other board members had already done. "I'll have to look into this," he said; folding the contract and putting it into his shirt pocket.

I had long since decided that, for whatever reason, Fandrich considered the school his sole responsibility. It was obvious that he greatly resented anyone else telling him what to do — including the sovereign state of Texas.

It would, in fact, be late in the summer before the contract would be returned to me, finally signed by all three members of the board. Even after signing it, though, Fandrich wasted no opportunity to make me aware that he had done so only because legislators in the state capital had forced him. His attitude convinced me that none of the wetbacks he employed in his mine could count on merit raises in the near future.

Each time I asked him if any progress was being made toward solving the accreditation problem, I was told only that the school board was looking into it. "Your job," Fandrich told me, "is to teach."

By the time the new school year began, it was clear that the accreditation problem was of secondary concern to the president of the school board. First, he wanted to have me fired.

In the beginning it was just a hunch on my part, a gut feeling brought on by a coolness in his voice and a sudden burst of interest in everything I did at the school. For the first time in my teaching career at Terlingua, I had somebody constantly looking over my shoulder, waiting for me to make a misstep — to fail to fly the flag or call roll or get my report cards out on time. Then as the year progressed, Ron Willard seemed to join forces with Fandrich in his watchdogging of my duties. There was nothing said or done outright which would permit me the luxury of knowing for certain they were set on getting me relieved of my job, but the feeling was there, like a thundercloud on the horizon.

It burst one evening when I had gone over to unlock the school so that the monthly school board meeting could be held. Shelly Katz, a photographer from Time magazine, had been visiting, taking photographs of the school and of Olga and myself for an article on people who had fled the city to seek a simpler life in rural America. His job done, he had invited us to drive up to Luna Vista Restaurant with him for a steak dinner. Inasmuch as such an extravagant night out is a rarity in our lives, it didn't please me to have to tell Shelly and Olga that I had to leave early to unlock the school, but we agreed to meet later at the Study Butte Cafe.

Shortly after I arrived Ron Willard showed up. We waited for quite some time and neither of the other board members arrived. Finally Pepper called to say everyone at his house had the flu and he wouldn't be able to make it. There was no word from Fandrich.

"Ron," I said, "I've already blown a pretty damn good steak dinner and I have a guest, so I suggest we turn out the lights, lock the door, and forget the meeting. Unless you want to have a one-man school board meeting."

He laughed and said, "Let's go home. Sorry to interrupt your dinner."

I was far from in a good mood as I drove away. Heading back toward the highway, I saw Joe Fandrich turn off and race toward the school. Recognizing my pickup as we approached each other, he began blinking his lights. Obviously he wanted me to stop. I kept driving. To hell with you, I thought. I was here on time, I did things by the book. You've got no gripe coming.

Apparently he felt he did. Olga and Shelly entered the cafe a few minutes later just in time to hear me say, "Joe, I don't want to listen to your shit!" and see him point his stubby finger at me and say, "Don't you ever cuss me in public again!" before storming out the door. A full-blown grade-school shouting match had thus ended. It was not one of my prouder moments.

Shelly tried to restore the light mood we had been sharing over steaks before the evening had turned sour. "I was hoping to get a few shots of you and the board president together," he said, "but I didn't bring any boxing gloves with me." Still angry, I showed little appreciation for his humor. "If you're going to use any pictures of me with that story," I said, "you'd better catch a fast plane to New York. If that guy has anything to do with it, I won't be the teacher here much longer."

In a matter of days I would be made aware that Fandrich was visiting the parents of each of my students, seeking any and all complaints they might have to offer.

The entire matter had taken on an unreal quality. As I sit thinking about it even now I can't for the life of me think how it all began; what little scratch began this festering into a painful sore. Since coming to Terlingua the few gripes voiced about my teaching had been over trivial, quickly solved matters. I was certain that virtually everyone in the community was pleased with the job I had done. I had upgraded the school in every way I possibly could. Quite frankly, I was proud of what I had accomplished. Yet here, all of a sudden, was the very real threat of being dismissed because of one man's disapproval.

"I came out here," I said to Olga as we sat up late one night discussing the onrushing problem, "to get away from all the petty, bureaucratic bullshit you see in the big schools. And now here I am right back in it. I think that's what disappoints me most about all this."

As soon as Fandrich had completed his round of visits to all the parents, he called a meeting of the school board which would be closed to the public. I had asked around and been told by several of the parents that a list of grievances had been prepared against me. The strongest indictment I was able to learn of was that Olga and I fixed ourselves a hot meal for lunch each day while the students ate the cold sandwiches they brought from home.

Olga blew a fuse when I told her of the charge. "You mean to tell me," she raved, stalking about the house as if she were addressing troops going into battle, "that they're thinking about firing you, the best damn teacher they've ever had, because I warm up a can of soup for us every day? A lousy can of soup? Their whole world is fixing to crash down around them with this accreditation business and they're wringing their hands over hot soup! God, I'd like to punch somebody in the nose!"

I couldn't help but be amused at her anger. I began to laugh. "You Greeks certainly have a temper," I said.

She finally calmed down and I outlined to her a plan I had come up with. It was far past time for me to quit standing by, waiting to see what was going to be my fate. The closed meeting the board had held was illegal, a direct violation of school board policy, and I was going to make sure everyone in the community was aware of the fact.

"What do you think of this?" I asked Olga, showing her a paper I had typed earlier. It read:

STATE OF TEXAS BREWSTER COUNTY

— PUBLIC PETITION—

WE THE UNDERSIGNED PARENTS AND MEMBERS OF THE COM-
MUNITY REQUEST THAT THE SUPERINTENDENT AND TERLIN-
GUA SCHOOL BOARD CALL AN OPEN MEETING FOR THE SOLE
PURPOSE OF DISCUSSING MR. JONES'S CONTINUING CONTRACT
FOR THE 1976-77 SCHOOL YEAR. WE REQUEST THAT THIS MEET-
ING BE HELD WITHIN THE NEXT SEVEN DAYS.

Beneath was one column for the signature of parents and another for other interested members of the community.

"I'm going to circulate this," I told her, "and your job is to get these filled out." I showed her a questionnaire I had also prepared. It had twelve questions:

1. Are you satisfied with your child's progress in school?
2. Are you satisfied with Mr. Jones as your child's teacher?
3. Do you have any complaints you would like to discuss here?
4. What do you like best about Terlingua School as a whole?
5. Would you like to see Mr. Jones continue to teach in this school?
6. What do you like best about Mr. Jones?
7. As you see it, what are Mr. Jones's weaknesses as a teacher?
8. Are you satisfied with the job the school board is doing?
9. What helpful suggestions would you make to the board to better help them in their job?
10. How would you feel if the board voted not to rehire Mr. Jones for the 1976–77 school year?
11. Would you be willing to stand up in Mr. Jones's defense in case of a public hearing concerning the matter of rehiring?
12. Would you be willing to write letters or personally talk to board members in Mr. Jones's defense in case the question of rehiring should arise?

"I want every parent to fill these out. Tell them to be as honest as they can. They all pretty well know what the situation is, so if they're for me, they'll help. If not, this gives them the opportunity to have their say."

Now it was Olga who was smiling. "This," she said, "is just a big ego trip for you, you know. You just want a bunch of people to write a lot of nice things about you and tell what a great teacher you are," she said.

"Well," I said, "under the circumstances I don't think it could hurt anything."

In a couple of days the petition had thirty-nine signatures, more than enough to justify the calling of an open board meeting. It was delivered to Joe Fandrich. Meanwhile, Olga was enthusiastically going about her job of getting the questionnaires completed.

"Listen to some of these," she said, motioning me into the chair behind my desk as class ended one afternoon. "I am very happy with Mr. Jones.... He gives great individual attention to the children... ." "My child has progressed more here than any other school he's ever attended... ." "He likes kids and works well with them... a man of kindness who cares about children... ."

"Mr. Jones, my husband, you have just been voted Teacher of the Year by the citizens of Terlingua. I congratulate you."

As I read over the answers the people had given to my questions, I felt a warmth that had been missing from my senses for quite some time. Though the testimonials had been blatantly solicited, they served as assurance to me that I had made some headway as a teacher here. They also caused me to remember something that, in my anger, disappointment, and discouragement of late, I had forgotten — that the silent majority can still be the loudest voice in a democracy.

"This is the one I like best," Olga continued, taking the questionnaires from my hand and thumbing through them. "This one is Mrs. Williams's. She doesn't even have any kids in school yet. Under the question 'How would you feel if the board voted not to rehire Mr. Jones for the 1976-77 school year?' she says, 'I not only would be very upset, I would be mad as hell.'"

Buoyed by the positive response to the questionnaires, I was still quite apprehensive about the forthcoming board meeting. The ultimate decision to retain me past the completion of the school year was in the hands of the three member school board. Glenn Pepper, I felt sure, would vote to rehire me. This entire mess had placed him in an awkward position because we had become close friends. I therefore had made every attempt to avoid him during the controversy in an effort to save him the discomfort of having to tell me he could not discuss the closed meeting with me. I was just as certain about Fandrich's vote. The battle lines had been clearly drawn.

Which left Ron Willard. In recent days I had felt even more strongly that he was siding with Fandrich. If so, it could, almost ironically, be he who would drop the ax. I could only hope that the public outcry — the answers to the questionnaires — might have an effect on their decision. One hundred percent of the parents had answered yes to the question of whether they were satisfied with their children's progress in school. One hundred percent had said they were satisfied with me as a teacher. One hundred percent had said they would like to see me continue to teach at the Terlingua School. And one hundred percent had indicated they would be upset — at least one "mad as hell" — if the school board voted not to rehire me.

There was nothing left to do but wait.

On the calendar in the bedroom Olga had circled April 27, 1976, and written D-Day alongside the date.

Daisy Adams stood near the door of the school, watching as the classroom filled far beyond its capacity. All the chairs I had put out were long since filled and late arrivals were standing along the walls, waiting for the meeting to be called to order. "This," Daisy whispered, "is far and away the largest attendance we've ever had at a school board meeting. Everybody who's not sick or stranded is here. Beats all. I've seen the time when we couldn't get six people out for an election. This is exciting!"

Olga, who had been sick to her stomach from worry all day, forced a smile. She had counted forty people in the room.

The people got their money's worth. Particularly if they liked surprise endings. Routinely, the meeting was called to order, and then Joe Fandrich took the floor. "Before we entertain any questions on the matter we are all here to discuss," he said, "I have an announcement I would like to make."

He spoke briefly of his tenure as a school board member, of the progress of the school, its importance to him and the community, and of difficulties legislators and other state officials had forced upon it.

"For a number of reasons, then," he concluded, "I have decided it is in the best interest of the school to submit my resignation, effective immediately."

As those in attendance sat in almost total silence, stunned by the unexpected turn of events, he walked briskly to the door, never so much as looking back.

Only after his truck's engine was heard to start up outside did people begin to voice their incredulity at what had transpired. Suddenly there was really nothing to meet about. Ben Simmons spoke briefly on his belief that crises often bring the people of a community closer together, and stated his conviction that things would now go smoothly again at the Terlingua School. "Now what we have to do is enlist a new member and call another meeting in the very near future to begin discussing a continuing contract for our teacher."

A few days later Ron Willard submitted his resignation. "I had planned to do it at the meeting when Joe did," he would later confide to fellow board member Pepper, "but I just didn't have the guts to in front of all those people. I think, though, that in view of the things that have happened lately, it would be in the best interest of the school if I stepped out. Besides, my wife nearly killed me when I got home from that meeting and told her I hadn't gotten around to resigning like I'd told her I was going to do."

In the days to come Daisy Adams and Ben Simmons would be elected to join Pepper on the school board.

After the school board meeting Olga and I remained at the school to rearrange the room in preparation for the next day's classes. We worked in silence for quite some time. As I was pushing desks back into place, Olga came over to me and put her arms around me. "Smile," she said. "You won." In a sense I suppose I had, but aside from the fact that I was now assured of remaining as teacher of the Terlingua School, it was a hollow victory. I wished it had never had to come to a winner-take-all showdown. "Honey," I said, "things really get crazy sometimes, don't they? I came out here expecting to get this job because I didn't think anybody else in the world would want it. I never thought I'd have to fight for it. But that's exactly what I've been doing. And I'd do it again if I had to. This is where I belong, where I have a chance to do something worthwhile, and it's going to take a helluva lot of Joe Fandrichs to convince me otherwise."

"The next time you get discouraged," Olga said, "I'm going to recite that little speech back to you."

"Promise me you'll do that," I said.

A few days after Ron Willard's resignation I stopped by his station to ask if he knew where the accreditation book was. He shuffled magazines and papers beneath the counter and found the book. "This is it, I think," he said.

"Ron," I asked, "do you know what's in it?"

"No," he said, "it's just some book Joe brought back at the beginning of the school year."

My worst suspicions were confirmed. The outline for the survival of the school had been sitting there under Ron Willard's counter for eight months. A year had gone by since the Texas Education Agency had advised us of what had to be accomplished, and despite Joe Fandrich's repeated insistence to me that everything was being taken care of, absolutely nothing had been done.

While Trent Jones and Cristina Farris work out a reading problem, young Bubba Stanton is having difficulty with his assignment. (PHOTO BY SKEETER HAGLER)

III

When I was a kid I hated school with a god-awful passion. I was bored to death with it and as a result was a blue ribbon example of what a brat a kid can be. It wouldn't surprise me to learn that I played a sizable role in more than one teacher's decision to seek another profession. Finally, my parents sent me off to military school in hopes that the strict discipline and the individual attention they would no doubt pay dearly for might help. I guess it did because suddenly one day learning became fun. It was a challenge instead of a bore. I found myself eager and receptive rather than hostile and stubborn. Today when I see kids in my class who are what some educators like to refer to as "slow learners," I see myself. Somehow, I've never managed to forget what a colossal pain in the ass the third grade can be.

— Trent Jones

When I took my first teaching job at Booker T. Washington in San Antonio, it was the policy of the school to adhere faithfully to all of the conventional methods of grading and disciplining students. If children talked or acted up in class they were made to stay inside during recess period; spankings were used as punishment for everything from chewing gum in class to throwing food at each other in the cafeteria; and the so-called real problem kids spent a great amount of their school time doing idiotic things like standing in the hall outside the principal's office or writing 100 lines beginning with "I will not... ."

More than once I found myself wondering if my primary duty was to try to teach kids or discipline them. Still, I tried all of the traditional methods-sometimes against my better judgment

— and quickly came to the conclusion that most of them were a gigantic waste of time. After my two years at Booker T., I decided that the cutups, the problem students, did not react to the standard discipline methods at all. In fact I found that they became even bigger headaches, thriving on the attention they received by getting spanked or being sent to stand out in the hall.

It further mystified me to find that a number of teachers even went so far as to use grades as a form of punishment. Often a problem kid would receive low marks not because he had done his work poorly but because he had caused some kind of problem to the teacher.

I realize that there is a need for some kind of discipline, some rules that must be enforced so the learning process won't be interrupted by a few disinterested students, but I am convinced that there are better ways of achieving it. Throughout my teaching career I have held to the belief that punishment breeds failure, that it breaks down desires and discourages a student from making an effort to really learn. I'm not talking about occasional discipline, but severe, constant punishment. A certain amount of punishment is necessary, unavoidable, but I've always felt my primary function was to help students learn, not deal out constant punishment to them.

When we moved to Terlingua one of the things I was most eager to try was something I called the praise method. What I wanted to do was place a strong emphasis on the positive aspects of a student's accomplishments instead of constantly dealing with the things he did wrong.

One of the first real opportunities I had to put this method of teaching to a strong test came about three years ago when a fourth-grader named Rodney, and his two older sisters, enrolled in the school. Their parents had moved to Terlingua Ranch and were selling real estate.

I can well remember my first impression of Rodney. He was a quiet kid who never looked anyone directly in the eye, never spoke unless spoken to, and was constantly looking around as if to see who might be looking at him for whatever reason.

As I was signing the children up, it became immediately obvious what Rodney's problem was. No sooner had I written their names on the registration forms than both of the sisters began telling me how poorly Rodney had done in the other schools they had attended and that the truth of the matter was that their little brother simply wasn't very smart. They told me that I shouldn't expect too much from Rodney. All this, mind you, while he was standing there, looking down at the floor with this embarrassed look on his face.

A few days later their mother stopped by the school and reemphasized what her daughters had told me. I listened to what she said, made no comment myself, and privately made up my mind to prove to everyone in that family that Rodney wasn't as dumb as they thought. My first chore, of course, would be to convince Rodney himself that he wasn't an impossible case. I would have to make him believe in himself despite what he was hearing at home. He had obviously not been allowed to succeed at anything. To his family he was a failure. To himself he was a failure. What I had to do was allow him to be a success.

So I very slowly began to work on him. At first he didn't want to do anything. He didn't even want to try. But I kept after him, making him do his work as best he could, and then I would pick something out to praise. Sometimes I had to look pretty hard to find something, but I praised him constantly. Over and over. I would tell him his work was wonderful and that I was very lucky to have him in my class.

It became apparent almost immediately that Rodney's greatest problem was reading. On the other hand, he did show some ability with numbers. So every day we would begin with his math lesson. He did it fairly well and therefore started the day off with a feeling of accomplishment and confidence. Having been successful with his math work and praised for that success, he would then strive to succeed in his other subjects for the remainder of the day.

Within a few months Rodney's personality began to undergo a complete change. He began to smile occasionally. He even laughed now and then. He began to do his work without so much prompting and was participating in class activities with the other students. Rodney was beginning to learn. And he was beginning to believe in himself.

Which is not to say the battle was over. He still had his sisters constantly telling him that he wasn't on a level with the other kids in the school. I tried to see to it that they didn't hound him about it at school, but I knew for a fact that they stayed on him pretty good at home. And the incredible thing about it all to me was the fact that evidently their mother continued to agree with her daughters. At school I could offer Rodney some measure of protection from the negative input. I tried to work on his sisters, pointing out to them that if they cared about their younger brother they could be a big help to him by not making him feel like a failure. In that respect I failed miserably. They were so convinced that their brother was dumb that they wouldn't even listen to me.

So what it boiled down to after a while was the fact that Rodney was something of a success at school but still a miserable failure at home.

I decided, then, to really lay it on thick, to build Rodney's confidence up to a point where he could stand on his own two feet regardless of what others said to him. Not only did I flatter him privately, but did so in front of the class whenever the opportunity arose. I wanted him to get to a point where he would tell his sisters, his parents, and the rest of the world that he was something.

With every passing day and every new word of praise, Rodney's classroom performance improved. Before long he was boldly telling people that he was getting smarter and was "one of Mr. Jones's best students." I'd never seen such a complete change of attitude in a child and, quite honestly, was feeling pretty proud of myself.

Until I started getting flack from his parents. They simply were not going to accept the fact that their son was doing so well. They challenged me about it, suggesting that the good grades he was bringing home were not really earned but, rather, just a gift from a pushover teacher who gave everyone good grades. They had made up their minds that Rodney was a dumb kid who had finally found a teacher who would simply give him good grades regardless. And sadly enough they let Rodney know how they felt about the matter.

I can only imagine the misery he must have gone through every afternoon, having to go home to such a totally negative environment — and how excited he was each morning to return to school and get away from it.

Rodney's case is not really that unique. In my years of teaching I've run across all too many cases like his. What it often boils down to is that the academic problems are not the fault of the student but the parents and sometimes even the teachers. Those people who are supposed to be a kid's strongest allies prove to be his biggest enemies.

A conversation I once had with another teacher perhaps best illustrates what I'm talking about. I was trying to explain my theory of praising a child to promote success and the teacher said to me, "What you're actually doing is lying to the kid. You're telling him that he's more than he really is. If a child is not as smart as the rest of the students, he simply has to learn to accept that fact and make the best of the situation."

That is what many of us in Terlingua would classify as garden variety bullshit. What he was telling me, in effect, was that there are smart kids and dumb kids and that they had damn well better learn to accept their proper place in society. As tragic as it may seem, I'm afraid that this train of thought typifies the way many parents and teachers feel about their students and children. I personally think they are dead wrong. How can you be lying to a kid by telling him that he is somebody special, that he is capable of doing wonderful, self-satisfying things?

Granted, some children are slower than others, but that doesn't mean they don't have the capability to learn and accomplish things at their own pace.

Toward this end I've found that sometimes praise alone isn't enough. I'm thinking now of Rocky and Robert Fierro, two brothers who attended the Terlingua School during my first two years of teaching here. They were, I was told by their parents and their previous teacher, very poor students and discipline problems. The report cards they brought along with them on their first day of class bore out both facts: Each had routinely failed every subject, and their conduct grades made one wonder how they were still walking the streets as free children. They made no bones about the fact that they hated school and teachers, not necessarily in that order.

Their parents were the opposite extreme from Rodney's. They stood up for their kids, refusing to admit that the blame should be placed anywhere but on the school system. It was a cop-out that teachers see all too often. The truth of the matter is that the parents were taking the easy way out.

They were ignoring the problems their kids were having, refusing to accept any of the responsibility. They offered no encouragement, didn't bother to help the boys with their homework, and, since they were people who enjoyed the night life, they saw nothing at all wrong with keeping their children out until all hours on school nights.

It was obvious from the outset, then, that getting Rocky and Robert to do homework would be a hopeless cause. If they were to be successful students and learn, they were going to have to do it all in the eight hours of class, five days a week.

I began the same praise method I had tried on Rodney and made some headway. Then I decided to try something different. Since they were so far behind — they were fourth graders but weren't able to do some of the work my second graders were handling — I decided to start repeating lessons until I felt they were on a level where they should be.

It was a tedious process at first, particularly with spelling, which was their worst subject. At the beginning of the week we would study the assigned words, and then work on them all through the week. Then on Friday I would give them a test. Their attitude toward tests was about on a par with their attitude toward teachers at first, but I repeatedly told them that tests were important because they enabled us to find how much we had learned. I told them that if they did poorly on a test it simply meant that they had to study a little harder to learn the material. What finally caught their attention, though, was my explanation to them that if they did badly on a test we would throw the bad grade out because it wasn't a bad grade that we were after; the goal was a good grade because it would signal the fact that the material had been learned.

So they took their spelling tests over and over until they

finally got all the words correct and received a good grade. It was a double victory — not only did they finally learn the words, they got a good grade to boot. With it all came the feeling of accomplishment that I wanted them to have.

And with it also came more criticism of my methods. One member of the community, upon hearing about my use of the repeat method for several of the students, made the comment that I was too liberal in my approach to teaching and that all I was doing was promoting laziness in the children. Some said that if I continued to stick with my repeat method all the students would adopt the attitude that they needn't bother to study for tests because they would be given a second, even a third, chance to make a good grade. I had made up my mind, though, long before I ever decided to try something new, that I wouldn't let outside opinion discourage me. The repeat method was working, and that was enough for me. Sure, some of the students had to take their tests several times to make A's or high marks, and, yes, there were a few who occasionally took advantage of the system, but overall the kids were learning. Once again I could see them beginning to enjoy learning, while the grades, which were no longer a threat to them, were becoming a secondary consideration. And that, I'm convinced, is what education should be. Students' efforts should be directed toward learning and the joys of learning rather than the accumulation of a bunch of meaningless grades on a piece of paper.

But you have a group of parents, a school board, and even a lot of students who expect to see those report cards every six weeks. What never ceases to amaze me are the cases like Rodney's where the parents are suspicious if the grades are too good and accuse the teacher of being too easy on the kids. Often at the same time there'll be those who insist you're grading too hard. As a teacher I've had to make up my mind who I'm going to please, who I'm trying to be successful with, the adults or the children: I've chosen to side with the kids.

It is my feeling that one of the most important jobs a teacher has is to create an atmosphere in which a child finds himself wanting to learn. If a student sincerely wants to learn, to pursue his natural curiosity, then half the teacher's battle is already won.

I like to keep the kids happy, and as everyone knows kids are happiest when they are playing or eating. So when I came to Terlingua I decided to experiment with breaking one of the most sacred rules of modern-day educational systems and allow students to chew gum in school and bring snacks to eat whenever they got hungry. What's so awful about chewing a stick of gum in the first place? What permanent damage could result from a kid having a couple of cookies or an apple while working on his math problems?

I just set down a few rules at the first of the year and explained that if they weren't followed the privilege would be taken away. Students were told they could snack or chew gum at any time they weren't working on an oral lesson, that they couldn't bother anyone else with their snacking, and that they should be neat about what they were doing. The children knew that this was a special concession that other schools didn't make, so the majority of them did their best not to abuse it.

One of the most positive aspects of the snack is that it allows the kids, particularly the younger ones, to eat when they're hungry. We generally have our snack after the morning physical education period, a time when a lot of the kids come back to the classroom a little hungry. The snack, eaten at their leisure while doing work at their desks, not only satisfies their hunger but also helps to relax them so they can better concentrate on their class work.

Yes, I have a few kids who don't follow the rules and have the privilege taken away from time. to time. But I can see no reason, because a few fail to follow the rules, to punish the majority who do.

I'm quite aware that the unique situation I have here in Terlingua has made it possible for me to do some things that might cause more orthodox educators to shake their heads. And I'm not trying to say that everything I've tried has worked. What I am saying, however, is that there are different ways to handle different situations. The simple fact that no two kids are exactly alike should be reason enough to realize that one catchall method of teaching is not going to satisfy the needs of everyone. I think when a teacher is able to determine the particular needs of a student and then gear his teaching for that student's benefit, success for everyone concerned is more likely.

But you have to be ready to accept the fact that there will be times when something that looks good in theory manages to fail miserably when put into practice. My career is living, breathing testimony to that. In fact, I'm probably the only teacher in the business to have had to form a search party to find a student who disappeared as a result of an educational brainstorm his teacher once came up with.

There was this particular youngster who, after having dropped out of school a couple of years before I came to Terlingua, finally decided to come back. He was already sixteen but somehow had managed to avoid learning to read more than a few simple words. As he had grown older his inability to read had become a great source of embarrassment to him and finally he had just chosen to quit school rather than face the daily jibes he received from the other students.

Now that he was back, obviously I was going to have to persuade him to make a crash effort to improve his reading before we could even come to a starting place in his schoolwork. So I tried to minimize the problem to him, telling him that it wouldn't be all that hard if he really worked at it. I told him that I was going to work with him but that he was going to have to do a lot of it on his own, doing reading outside the classroom. I went into a rather long-winded story about how Abe Lincoln had, as a boy, successfully taught himself to read by going out into the woods and sitting under a tree during the day and then by the light of the fireplace at night. "Who knows?" I said. "You might even grow up to be president someday."

Looking back, I'm afraid I overdid it a little.

A couple of days later he didn't show up for school. His father came that afternoon to pick him up and was surprised to learn that his son was not there. We began calling around, checking at the cafe and the service station — everywhere we could think he might be playing hooky — but couldn't find him. By late afternoon the boy's parents were in a state of near panic and had called the highway patrol. There was talk about summoning a helicopter from Alpine to begin a search.

In the meantime a group of men had volunteered to begin combing the desert around the boy's home. I stayed at the school just in case for some reason he might show up there or the highway patrol had anything to report by telephone. There was but a hint of daylight remaining when the boy's father came by to tell me that his son had been found.

His face reflected neither the relief nor the joy I would have expected in such a situation.

"Where did you find him?" I asked.

"Out in the goddamn desert, sitting under a mesquite tree, reading a book," the father said.

As I said, you can't win them all.

Blindfolded Wick Fowler
judges a contestant's chili
Wick was a past first prize winner
and creator of "Two-Alarm Chili."
(PHOTO BY PETER KOCH)

IV

Lord, God, you know us old cowhands is forgetful. Sometimes, I can't even recollect what happened yesterday. We is forgetful. We just know daylight from dark, summer, fall, winter, and spring. But I sure hope we don't never forget to thank you before we eat a mess of good chili.

We don't know why, in your wisdom, you been so doggone good to us. The heathen Chinese don't have no chili, never. The Frenchmen is left out. The Russians don't know no more about chili than a hog knows about a sidesaddle. Even the Mexicans don't get a good whiff of chili unless they live around here.

Chili eaters is some of your chosen people, Lord. We don't know why you're so doggone good to us. But, Lord God, don't never think we ain't grateful for this chili we are about to eat. Amen.

— Chili prayer of old-time Negro range cook Bones Hooks

Hondo Crouch's recipe for his famous armadillo chili: "Take one medium-sized armadillo. Add other things. Save the shell."

It is difficult to judge how Texas history will deal with the World Championship Chili Cook-off which has been held in Terlingua annually for the past ten years. But if I had to guess I'd say it will probably be catalogued somewhere alongside the fact that the Texas legislature, in a flight of fancy, once passed a resolution applauding Jack the Ripper for his untiring efforts to help curb the population explosion and, more recently, the fact that the governor, Dolph Briscoe, appointed a man five years dead to the state Health Advisory Committee.

You have to understand that, for all of the frivolity that surrounds it, the business of cooking chili is no lightly taken matter to many Texans. Lyndon Johnson, while exiled from the Texas hill country and living in the White House, is said to have always made sure that ample amounts of Lady Bird's Pedernales River Chili was put aboard Air Force One along with other items of world importance when he was traveling. White House chef Henry Haller was careful to always freeze it beforehand so that he'd be able to scrape the fat off before it was served to the President. Ol' Lyndon loved his chili, but not swimming in grease.

The cook-off is a fun-and-games kind of madness we find ourselves thrust into every October. The attitude Olga and I have about it reminds me of the way my grandmother used to feel about us kids coming to visit her for a weekend: "I really love to see you come," she used to say, "and I really love to see you go."

On that single, crazy weekend the old ghost town comes back to life, filled with the twangy, nasal sound of country music, all night dancing, beer drinking, chili cooking, and various forms of general hell raising that sane people wouldn't normally consider doing in the privacy of their own homes.

They come from all over the United States, in cars and campers, buses, and several chartered planes which land at the Terlingua Ranch's private airstrip. The purpose of the two-day gathering is supposedly to determine who will reign for the forthcoming year as the best chili con carne cook in the world, though I have to say that somewhere along the line the culinary aspect of the cook-off seems to have been lost in the shuffle of wet

T-shirt contests, fist fights, two-day drunks, and tall-tale telling the likes of which I've never before experienced.

All in all, it's definitely not your normal weekend in Terlingua. In fact, it is a time when a number of the local residents find an urgent need to get away for a couple of days, to pay long-overdue visits to relatives or tend to some distant business that seems to call for attention in October each year. The cafes and groceries, however, keep their doors open longer hours than usual for the simple economic reason that the sudden jump in population enables them to sell more beer, ice, potato chips, cheeseburgers, and canned goods in forty-eight hours than they normally do in three months. Actually, there are several businesses that manage to survive only as a result of the business they are able to do during the cook-off each year.

The World Championship Chili Cook-off is the brainchild of a collection of eccentric Dallas businessmen who belong to a group they call the Chili Appreciation Society International. Prior to 1967 they would gather for irregular but well-attended "chili banquets," there to toast their favorite food (which recently was proclaimed the official state dish of Texas by an act of the Texas legislature), share recipes, and engage in hearty fellowship. One of the big movers in the organization was a *Dallas Morning News* columnist named Frank Tolbert whose book *Bowl of Red* was and still is considered the bible of chili aficionados.

It was, then, a basically harmless group until the late humorist writer H. Allen Smith got into the act. A piece he had done for *Holiday* magazine, immodestly titled "Nobody Knows More

About Chili Than I Do," sent the Dallas chili establishment into a frothing rage. That some easterner would have the gall to make such an outrageous claim in print, no less, was not something that could go unnoticed. The Chili Appreciation Society, immediately upon being made aware of Smith's boast, called an emergency meeting and decided that a challenge should be issued without waste of time. Tolbert himself, no doubt seeing the very real possibility of promoting his own journalistic efforts on chili, launched into a printed tirade against Smith in his newspaper column.

Actually, unbeknown to Smith who would later view himself as the centerpiece of the whole insanity and write a book about what he liked to refer to as The Great Chili Confrontation, he was a late entry in the chili derby. Plans had in fact been under way for some time for a cook-off that would match Wick Fowler, chief chili cook of the Dallas organization, and Dave Chasen, Elizabeth Taylor's favorite chili cook who headquartered in Beverly Hills.

Chasen, however, fell ill at about the same time Smith's *Holiday* magazine piece hit the newsstands. Fowler, an Austin journalist and founder of the Caliente Chili Company which provides Texas grocery shoppers with One-, Two-, and Three-Alarm Chili preparation, made the public statement that, hell, yes, he'd just as soon go head-on with some eastern dude as a Hollywood tutti-frutti. The challenge was thus issued, and Smith damn near busted his equipment accepting.

The site of the cook-off was an easy decision. Dallas lawyer David Witts, a member of the local Chili Society, was at the time the owner of the ghost town of Terlingua and offered his 600 acres for the event — provided he could serve as one of the judges.

Just over 1000 people attended the original cook-off, there to argue the virtues of eastern versus southwestern chili and cheer their respective cookers on. Amid all the ballyhoo and fun the cook-off ended in a draw. One judge voted for Smith, another for the cherub-faced Fowler, and the third, Terlingua owner Witts, passed out and was thus unable to render a tie-breaking verdict. The reasons offered for his default varied: too much desert sun, too little water, too much Scotch, or somebody's bad chili had rendered his taste buds inoperative and caused him to lapse into a temporary coma.

Attending writers from publications ranging from *Sports Illustrated* to something called the *Wretched Mess Press* joined reporters from both wire services in a dash for their typewriters so they might inform the waiting world of the news. It's been going on ever since. In recent years the crowds have grown to as many as 15,000 people coming from all over the United States, Japan, England, and Mexico. The format of the competition has since been altered to include a dozen or so entrants, each having qualified by winning other chili cook-offs in their home states or areas. In 1975, Allegani Jani McCullough became the first woman to earn the championship after years of being barred. It was Jani, in fact, who had masterminded a formal protest of women cooks a year earlier, having leaflets saying "No Chili, No Thrilli" dropped from a rented plane onto the largely male chauvinist gathering.

This year's cook-off, quite frankly, was something of a let down. For the first time in its existence someone tried to bring some order to the event, and, secondly, one of the most interesting people who had been involved in it from its origin was missing.

Hondo Crouch, a merry old man who wore western attire, sported a snow-white beard, and laid claim to one of Terlingua's old adobe buildings years ago and christened it the Hondo Hilton, had died just a few weeks before the event. Olga and I had looked forward to seeing him and listening to his outrageous stories and the Mexican ballads he sang.

The leadership of the cook-off — if it ever had such a thing — has now been passed almost solely to Tolbert, since both Wick Fowler and H. Allen Smith have also died. While Smith had little to do with the event after his initial participation, he had moved to Alpine to live the last several years of his life and seemed to be able to keep the locals stirred up pretty regularly with his articles.

With Hondo missing, a lot of the color was drained from the event. He was owner and self-proclaimed mayor of a little Texas hill country town called Luckenbach which had an official population of six and, as he so often reminded us, was closed on Wednesdays. His little town was a thriving community on weekends, however, as young people from Austin, San Antonio, and Houston flocked to Luckenbach to drink beer and participate in the variety of lunacies Hondo conjured up. He staged events like the First Second Annual Luckenbach World's Fair, a Luckenbach Film Festival (at which only home movies were shown on a bed sheet in the old clapboard dance hall in town), and a Hug-In each Valentine's Day.

It was Hondo, I think, who best described the chili cook-off: "A chili cook-off," he said, "is an absurd thing. And Terlingua, Texas, is an absurd thing. So, when you put a chili cook-off in Terlingua you have an absurd absurdity."

Paul Vonn, it should be here noted, is not a man who tolerates the absurd. Having gained ownership of the ghost town, the sixty-eight-year-old, pony tailed Vonn declared martial law on his town and its guests. "Boozers and potheads," he announced, "will be arrested. We're either going to clean this thing up or kill it this time around."

The latter would, to my way of thinking, be the easiest thing to do. In fact, the idea of cleaning up the chili cook-off was one of the worst I ever had.

My first year in Terlingua I decided it might be a good idea if my students volunteered to clean up after the cook-off and I suggested to the officials of the event that we would do so if they would take up a donation from the crowd for our efforts. Fund raising projects aren't all that easy to come by in the middle of nowhere and I thought sure this would be a gold mine, what with everybody having a good time drinking and in general high spirits.

To make a long story short, we loaded and hauled off something like fourteen pickup-loads of trash the week after that cook-off — not really making a dent in the mess, and got a grand total of $50 for our efforts. From that time on we've satisfied our need to participate by doing signs saying "Please Don't Litter" and placing them around the camping area. Needless to say, they go largely ignored.

Vonn, however, was dealing in morals in his cleanup campaign and enlisted the help of what looked like half the law enforcement agencies in the Trans-Pecos to help him. On the first day of the cook-off he made it clear that law and order would prevail: no drinking after midnight, no loud music after midnight, no pot smoking, and no drunk driving. For those who chose to ignore the rules there was a large portable cage that had been hauled in to serve as a temporary jail. In a scene straight out of a bad movie, over 175 law officers — state troopers, Texas Rangers, U.S. marshals and deputies, federal narcotics agents, and off-duty policemen from Alpine and El Paso — marched into town six abreast as Vonn issued his ultimatum.

Tolbert, greatly upset over the grim military atmosphere that was threatening his chili celebration, approached Vonn and asked, "Why didn't you invite the national guard out for maneuvers? That would have been a real show of force. And you could have hired a few Department of Safety helicopters —"

At that moment a DPS helicopter appeared on the horizon, flying low, headed in the direction of the World Championship Chili Cook-off.

Charlie Fowler, nephew of the late Wick who had helped start the whole mess, stood in the back of his pickup, watching as cars, vans, trucks, campers, and mobile homes bearing license plates from all over the nation poured into Terlingua. The crowd would finally be estimated at 4000.

Soon makeshift campsites were cropping up all around with tents and sleeping bags everywhere. Across the highway the jail had been put in place and was already occupied by several people who never even made it to their campsites, having been arrested en route for drunken driving. Clearly it wasn't going to be the same old hell-raising, all night drinking and singing cook-off we had all learned to tolerate if not appreciate.

Fowler, the designated scorekeeper for this year's cook-off, joined Tolbert in his displeasure at Vonn's actions. "You've got to be leery of any sixty-some-odd-year-old sonofabitch who wears his hair in a ponytail, I always say. He says he's afraid of hippies. What I think is he's about as flaky as they come."

I did not seek an opportunity to disagree with Fowler's observation.

Olga wanted to see if anyone was staying in the Hondo Hilton, so we walked over to where it stood and found that it had been converted into a honeymoon cottage for Allegani Jani and her new husband, singer-writer Lee McCullough. The couple had been married a week earlier as the highlight of the Ma Ferguson Memorial Women's Chili Cook-off which had been sponsored by the Hell Hath No Fury Society in Luckenbach. They told us that instead of rice, those attending the wedding had thrown pinto beans.

Jani, as a defending champion, was again entered, along with a couple of other women — Ruby Smith, the Oklahoma State champion, and Beth Moon of Fort Worth who won the Texas title while Jani was busy getting married.

Actually, the Terlingua cook-off had had a wedding of its own the previous year when Nancy Fowler Sebastian, niece of Wick

Fowler, and Peter George Kleck decided to be married in what remains of the Terlingua chapel. Hallie Stillwell, a colorful justice of the peace from Alpine, conducted the ceremony wearing a crown labeled "Chili Queen" and a necklace of green chili peppers. The bride carried a bouquet of chili peppers, the men wore chili pepper boutonnieres, and there was a little "pepper girl" in attendance rather than the traditional flower girl. Olga said she thought it was a rather clever idea.

Someone played "Here Comes the Bride" on the guitar as Nancy walked down the aisle, and when Hallie asked who was giving the bride in marriage, her dad stepped forward and bellowed, "Maw 'n' me."

For their wedding trip the new bride and groom crossed the Rio Grande on burros to Boquillas, Mexico. I never heard from them again, though I imagine somewhere in the mass of humanity they were on hand for this year's cook-off.

The traditional Friday night dance was scheduled to begin as soon as the sun set, but, having swallowed enough dust, Olga and I decided to go on home. I was later told that a couple of dozen people were hauled out of the dance and placed in the tiger cage by Texas Rangers. One had committed the crime of giving a beer away past the stroke of midnight, and several were jailed, if you can believe it, for disorderly conduct. Hell, that's what the chili cook-off is all about.

I found the whole thing hilarious. For years Harold Wynne, a seventy-five-year-old ranch foreman with one eye who also served as the local police chief, had shouldered the entire burden of keeping the affair down to a mild roar. Aside from several hundred fist fights and as many as 15,000 drunks, he had never had any trouble.

Despite the frowns and angry warnings of Vonn's troops, the night wore on. There was, it was reported, a lot of drinking, hollering, hugging, falling down, and throwing up. I'm glad we were home.

The morning of the actual cook-off dawned cold. Up in the Davis Mountains snow had fallen, and in Alpine the nighttime temperature had dipped to 20 degrees.

While I frankly couldn't have cared less who would reign as the world's champion chili cook, I was interested to see how Vonn's army handled the events of the day. And Olga had her heart set on getting one of the World Championship Chili Cook-off T-shirts she had seen somebody wearing. So we returned to the ghost town Saturday.

By midmorning the bright sunshine had chased the chill from the air and the fifty or so official entrants were setting up their big black kettles along Dirty Woman Creek.

One was a dapper-looking man named Phillips Beckley, who had flown in from Mexico in his DC-3. "I'm here under orders from Hector Moyogo, the governor of the state of Durango," said Beckley, who is the owner of the huge Santa Cruz Mining Company in Durango. "The governor believes it is time for the title to be taken back to Mexico where chili started." He was going to win, he claimed, by using a magic ingredient — a plant called ancho.

There was also an engineering professor from Southern Methodist University who introduced himself as Smoke Mouth Jack Harley — in my academic experience I've never met a professor with a name like Smoke Mouth — and claimed that cooking chili and growing house plants had one thing in common: You have to talk to both of them for best results. Thus he stirred and added ingredients, talking in a low muffled voice all the while. He insisted that he had spent thirty years in an SMU laboratory experimenting with chili and had finally been successful in improving on a recipe his grandmother, Mrs. Addie Harley, had once used to prepare chili for outlaw Sam Bass at the point of a gun. The chili so satisfied Bass, Harley said, that he fell asleep and was ultimately captured.

As we wandered along the row of cooks we saw people making chili with everything from armadillo to pinecones. A group of Tigua Indians from a reservation near El Paso had made the pilgrimage to enter and drew a considerable crowd of onlookers as they prepared their entry. Jose Sierra, the tribal governor, didn't bother to use a ladle, instead kneading the bright red mush with his bare hands. As we stood watching he pulled his arms from the pot, drenched to the elbows, and tasted his brew. He expressed immediate displeasure and began cubing more peppers and dumping them into the pot.

While the cooks continued their preparations in anticipation of the judging, a variety of other contests were under way. A very healthy young lady who was a student at Texas Tech University won the wet T-shirt contest hands down (and shoulders arched back), and some man with a gaping hole in the seat of his pants was named Mr. Terlingua. The applause he drew didn't rival that of the wet T-shirt champion.

In virtually every crowd you stepped into you could hear angry criticism of Paul Vonn's heavy-handed action. The lone person I encountered who offered support of Vonn was his son-in-law, Mike North, who had cornered a group of newsmen flown in to cover the event and was telling them how the intervention of the many peace officers at the cook-off had prevented any number of fist fights the night before. A reporter, who obviously was doing far more participating than reporting, looked at Mike, took a long drag from his beer, and said, "Who gives a shit? Hell, I got into one of the best fist fights of my life right over yonder this time last year. That's part of it. What your Mr. Bonn or Vonn or whatever the hell his name is has done is fuck up one damn good chili cook-off."

The last time I saw Mike he was wandering about with a frustrated look on his face, keeping constant company with a couple of Texas Rangers who looked as if they had enjoyed about all the chili cook-off they could stand.

Eventually, though, despite Vonn and his army and his tiger-cage jail, the big moment arrived. The judges began their march along the row of kettles, sampling the chili. That accomplished, they returned to the shelter of the old general store and compared notes.

The winner was a man named Albert Agnor, Texas A & M Class of '47, from Marshall, Texas (which also gave us such celebrities as former New York Giants quarterback Y. A. Tittle and actress Susan Howard), who admitted to the crowd that the secret of his culinary success was farkleberries — blackberries that grew on farkle bushes. Everyone seemed satisfied with his explanation, though I have serious doubts as to the existence of a farkleberry anywhere on this or any other planet.

The promoters of the event made no bones about the fact that this year's chili cook-off was a bust. The blame was unanimously placed on Vonn.

David Witts, who I understood had nearly come to blows with Vonn the night before, indicated that the event might be held on his ranch next year instead of the ghost town.

Said Fowler, "Maybe it's time to move it anyway and, leave the ghosts of Terlingua in peace."

There are a number of living, breathing residents who would appreciate that same consideration.

γ

❀ ❀ ❀

No person, especially a little kid, is going to concentrate for very long if he's hungry. Besides, a little peanut butter on a math paper never hurt anybody.

—Trent Jones

Trent is not sleeping well. His body rests but his mind doesn't.
—A late November entry in Olga's diary

The chili cook-off having at last been put to rest for another year, Tony Shemroske, a talented New Orleans artist who has been struck with a fascination for both chili and the Texas Trans-Pecos, agreed to stay over for a few days and come by the school to give the students a lesson in watercolor painting. "Hell, I've never even taken a lesson, much less given one," he said, "but it might be fun. Even if the kids don't learn anything, they'll probably appreciate not having to do their multiplication tables or diagram sentences for a while. I'll be there."

Our friendship with Tony is one of the better things to result from my infrequent visits to past cook-offs. A couple of years ago we met and he had come to the house to escape the all night hell-raising. He seemed genuinely fascinated by our little school and asked endless questions about my decision to teach here instead of fighting my way up the professional ladder until I finally managed to arrive at an administrative position in some school in one of the state's larger school districts.

Now that I've come to know him better, it occurs to me that these were rather strange questions for him to have asked. For years he had worked at an eight-to-five job as a government employed draftsman, then one day made the sudden decision to walk away from the job, the security, the regular paychecks and company benefits, and pursue a livelihood as a pen-and-ink and watercolor artist. He purchased a van which now serves as his home on wheels and, as he likes to put it, he "goes wherever the inspiration is." "The only way I could ever hope to do that," he points out, "was to get away from offices and time clocks and piped in music and the worn out faces of guys who had given twenty-five boring years to the company."

Much of that inspiration he sought has been found in the ruins of Terlingua and the Mexican villages across the river. His drawings of the old adobe remains of the ghost town, the Lajitas Trading Post, and street scenes from Boquillas now hang in some of the most fashionable homes and office buildings in the state.

At last year's cook-off he donated for auction a drawing he had done of one of the old Perry mines, with the stipulation that the money it earned be given to the school. Needless to say, I was delighted when C. V. Wood, the eccentric millionaire from California who gained national fame not too long ago when he bought the London Bridge and had it reassembled in Arizona, bid $200 for the drawing.

"He'll mail you a check," Tony assured me, "as soon as he gets back home." I immediately began visualizing a long planned rock patio which would rim the school, financed at last by this windfall. The patio, I'm happy to report, was finally built as the new school was being completed, but unless millionaire Wood's check arrives in today's mail I must point out he is now slightly over a year delinquent in his payment.

Tony did visit the school as he'd promised. And as he spoke to the students, doing a brightly colored field of flowers as he talked, there was a quiet attentiveness in the room which I must admit I had never succeeded in commanding. Much of what he had to say was a bit too technical for some of the younger students, but their fascination with his ability to make a picture come to life on a blank sketch pad kept every eye admiringly focused on the silver haired artist.

His picture and lecture completed, he invited the students to come to the front of the room in small groups and patiently instructed each in the art of drawing a daisy.

Bubba Staton, a first-grader who can generally be found climbing all over his desk or running about the room interrupting the studies of the other children, wiggled impatiently as he awaited his turn with one of Tony's brushes. A youngster with considerable artistic ability and an enthusiastic interest in the field, he proudly called Tony's attention to one of his pictures that I'd framed and hung on the wall of the classroom. "I'm going to be an artist too, as soon as I grow up," he said matter-of-factly to his visiting instructor. Tony paid admiring attention to the picture hanging on the wall. "Well, sir," he said, handing a brush to the delighted six-year-old, "I'd say you're off to a pretty good start already. I was a lot older than you before anyone thought enough of one of my paintings to hang it on the wall."

Tony Shemroske's visit to the class was one of those events the students would talk about for weeks to come. New dedication to art lessons was clearly evident. I had thoroughly enjoyed watching the reactions of the students as they took their turns at trying to impress Tony with their artistic efforts. Dead serious, biting bottom lips or sliding tongues to the sides of frowning mouths, they did their level best to imitate the smooth, graceful brush strokes they had seen him use earlier. Before leaving, he would see to it that each of the students had completed a watercolor to take home to show to his parents.

It was one of those delightful kinds of days that seem to end all too soon.

When our next visitor came, however, I silently questioned whether the day would ever be over.

Since Brewster County Judge Sam Thomas, *ex officio* superintendent of our school, had called from Alpine to advise us of the upcoming visit in a few days from a Texas Education Agency inspector, a crash program of spit polishing the school had been under way. Windows were washed, blackboards cleaned, desks set in order, shelves dusted, and floors swept and reswept. If there had been a cot in the building I suspect our visitor would have been able to bounce a quarter off it, so thorough was the preparation for our inspection.

"How long do you expect he'll be here?" Olga asked as she hurried about the kitchen preparing ham sandwiches and deep frying doughnuts.

"Too long." I had to pick this day of all days in my life to oversleep after a tossing-and-turning night and was not yet the best of company.

"He's just coming to inspect the school, not blow it up," Olga reminded. "Anyway, if he's here around lunchtime you can bring him over to the house and have sandwiches. I'll leave a pot of coffee to go with the doughnuts."

I smiled. If the way to an accreditation inspector's heart was through his stomach, Olga was going to see to it that the advantage went to the Terlingua School. The ham which she had slowly baked all night filled the room with a pleasing sweet aroma. I almost developed an appetite but instead chose to make do with a cup of coffee. "I'm really nervous," I said.

Olga set a cup in front of me. "I know," she said.

We were out on the school grounds for physical education and had just chosen sides for a baseball game when Jack Mayberry, an auditor for the Texas Education Agency, drove up. As he approached I sized him up as if he were some threatening sparring partner instead of a man who had arrived to simply carry out the responsibilities of his job. He was just under six feet, stocky, probably in his early fifties; his hair was thinning and he wore glasses. I decided I could probably have taken him in two rounds.

"Got any future major-leaguers out here?" he said as he approached, smiling and extending his hand.

"You must be Jack Mayberry, the big-league scout," I replied as we shook hands.

"Afraid not." His laughter was reassuring but brief. As we stood on the playground, watching the students, he wasted no time outlining to me the things he would need to accomplish during his visit. He would need to look over the building, check my inventory of supplies and teaching aids, inspect our textbooks and library, and ask me a number of questions which were printed on a form he carried on his clipboard. "I'm afraid there are a number of questions," he said, "so your classroom schedule might be disrupted pretty badly, but this was the only time I could get here. I hope it won't cause too much of a problem."

I explained to him that Olga had taken our two girls to spend the day with Mrs. Acosta so that Olga could watch, the class for whatever time necessary. "I've already given out assignments," I said.

A cheerful man, friendly and courteous, he spoke with several of the students as he walked about the classroom, taking note of the size of the building, the number of desks, and the amount of storage space. Obviously, his was a trained eye, one that had doubtless performed the same routine innumerable times during his career.

His tour completed, he joined me in the back of the room. "Suppose," he suggested, "we just talk for a while before we get to the specific questions I'll need you to answer. Maybe you can brief me on what you and your school board have accomplished in regard to meeting accreditation requirements to this point."

I told him of the curriculum guides that were being prepared, and of the tentative plan to reevaluate the tax structure for the district. I offered to show him my progress on the writing of the school board policies and expressed to him the community interest in helping in any way possible to meet the necessary requirements. He listened with interest as I explained the problems with the previous school board which had caused the long delay in taking initial action on some of the requirements. There was, I assured him, not a single item on the list that wasn't being dealt serious attention.

"Is it your honest feeling," he asked, "that the children of Terlingua would be better served by attending this school instead of being consolidated into the Alpine system?"

"I think it would be a disaster to consolidate. The distance alone creates a tremendous problem. And the kids in this school are doing well. Many of them, in fact, are working at a level far beyond what they would normally be because of the relatively small enrollment. Here I've got time to work with them on a one-on-one basis instead of just passing out papers and having them handed back to be graded. I realize we're a long way from Austin and that you people have far greater problems to deal with than the accreditation of a little one-room school out in Terlingua, Texas, but here it is the most important thing in the community. The kids love this school. So do I. And it's important to the parents of Terlingua. That's why we're doing everything in our power to meet the requirements given us."

"I can appreciate your feelings, Mr. Jones," he said. "On the other hand, several of the smaller schools similar to yours have already resigned themselves to consolidation. They simply looked at the alternatives, saw the overwhelming difficulty of meeting all the requirements, and have advised us they will close at the end of the year."

Olga had returned from taking Anna and Cassandra to Mrs. Acosta's and I suggested we walk over to the house for a cup of coffee while she took over the class.

Sampling one of Olga's doughnuts, Mayberry looked over his questionnaire. "Do you have a forty-five-minute planning period at some point during your teaching day?" he asked.

"No, I'm with the students from the time school begins until the day's over. But if necessary I could easily tack a planning period onto the beginning or end of the day."

"I'm afraid the requirement is that it has to be done at some time during the course of regular school hours."

"Aren't there exceptions to the rules, for exceptional situations?"

"Mr. Jones, I hope you'll understand that I'm not here to pass any judgments, but merely to conduct an inspection. But, to answer your question: No, there are no exceptions to be found in the Texas Education Code."

As the day went on, the picture Jack Mayberry painted grew dimmer and dimmer. I began to realize that there was far more work left to be done than I had ever contemplated. The list of minor requirements alone that were not being met to Mayberry's satisfaction seemed to grow with every question he asked, every area into which he probed.

No, we did not maintain a well-equipped laboratory for science instruction to seventh- and eighth-graders. "But I don't even have any seventh-graders this year and just three eighth graders," I explained.

No exceptions.

Our budget for supplies and equipment was only $250 annually, or approximately $11 per student, whereas in the larger schools almost $400 is spent on each child. "But we don't want for anything. If we need something, I'm free to go over to Morrison's Department Store in Alpine and pick it up. We see to it that the kids have everything they need."

No exceptions.

My college transcript and teaching certificate were not on file in the school building as required by law. "Olga keeps all our papers in a drawer in the house. It's just a few steps away."

No exceptions.

He found our library, our storage space and shelving, still inadequate; several textbooks I was using were from last year's list recommended by the Texas Education Agency; the minutes of our school board meetings were not properly signed and recorded. And on top of all the relatively minor shortcomings, he had only my word that some of the more serious matters were being dealt with.

Mayberry must have read the look of discouragement on my face. "I sincerely hope you won't take any of what I'm saying personally. In fact, I'd like for you to know that I'm very impressed with the job you're doing here. And I admire you for wanting to work toward keeping this school open. It's just that the state of Texas insists that its schools are run by the letter of the law with —"

"No exceptions. I know." He smiled and nodded.

"It would be helpful," I said, "if you could give me an honest evaluation of how we stand on this thing. A lot of the things you've pointed out can be corrected right away. And we'll have the new building on the grounds shortly. That should enable us to take care of the lack of space... ."

"There are some borderline situations," he explained, "which I won't be responsible for making a decision on, but I'll have to include them in my report. For instance, Mr. Jones, with the number of students you have and the eight grade levels you are teaching at, it would be my guess that you will be required to hire another teacher. At least an aide who can assist you part-time."

"Olga helps me some, but she gets no salary," I explained. "We don't have the money to pay an assistant right now."

"Therein lies your biggest problem as I see it," he said. "I saw no evidence of any kind of financial plan that insures the continued operation of the school while I was visiting in Judge Thomas's office. I realize there is talk about a raise in taxation, but there is absolutely nothing to assure that it will come about. Before I left Austin I did some research and found that this school district has been habitually late with submitting reports, filing of budgets and audits. Your last audit, for instance, was supposed to have been received in Austin last December, but I could find no indication that it has yet been filed."

He had, I felt, finally stabbed at the heart of many of our problems.

Regularly since I'd been in Terlingua I'd received calls from various departments of the Texas Education Agency asking why particular forms had not been filled out and returned. Several times, in fact, threats of cutting off state money to the school had been hinted at if the forms were not immediately sent. For the first couple of years I would simply tell the caller that I was only the teacher and did not handle such matters, and refer them to Judge Thomas.

When, however, some state funding was actually held up because of his refusal to meet deadlines, I decided to ask any other callers to simply send whatever forms needed to be filled out directly to me. After Jack Mayberry's inspection, I was convinced that Judge Thomas wasn't likely to change his habits, and with the accreditation problem hanging over our heads we could ill afford any more enemies in Austin. So I wrote to the TEA attempting to explain the situation, apologized for Sam Thomas's past failures, and emphasized again that I would be happy to assume the responsibility of handling the paper work for our school district in the future.

Now, the only forms Judge Thomas sees are those that require his signature, and almost without exception I get a call or a letter reminding me that the deadline has passed without those forms having been received. Thomas had, in fact, even been the subject of an editorial in the Alpine Avalanche. It questioned why the dockets showed 212 cases not yet given trial dates and asked what the judge was doing to earn his $12,720-a-year salary. Thomas answered the charges in the next day's edition with the same answer he had so often given to me: "I admit I should have gotten around to it sooner. I'm going to get right on it."

"Is it possible," I asked Mayberry now, "for the school board to be given Judge Thomas's administrative duties so that we can see to it that things are done on time?"

He shook his head. "I'm aware of some of the problems you've had in this particular area but, no, the Education Code states that the job must be handled by a qualified professional. In our system the presiding county judge serves as the ex officio superintendent for common school districts like yours. It's quite possible that Judge Thomas would welcome the opportunity to relinquish that duty if there were someone qualified who could take it over. Obviously, though, you have a shortage of candidates here in Terlingua."

"Mr. Mayberry," I answered, "we've got a shortage of a lot of things in Terlingua. Problems, however, don't seem to be one of them at the moment."

"I'm afraid I have to agree with you. I'm sorry I can't paint you a better picture. The honest truth is you are facing a demanding uphill battle if you decide to work toward accreditation. If you and your board have already come to that decision, I'll make a note of it in my report and in all likelihood another visit will be necessary in the spring to see what you've accomplished."

"Your report isn't going to be very favorable, is it?" "Again let me emphasize that the decision to grant or deny you accreditation does not rest with me," he said in preface, "but, since you asked and I feel you deserve an answer, no, I'm afraid it won't be a very favorable report."

With that he gathered his papers. "Please thank your wife for the sandwiches and the doughnuts," he said.

I walked with him to the car, watched as he drove away, and turned back toward the school. Olga stood in the doorway, waiting.

"What did he say?" she asked.

"He said he loved your ham sandwiches, but he's not too crazy about anything else around here."

She looked away from me, searching some invisible point out on the mountainside, saying nothing. A solitary tear slowly slid down the side of her face that I could see. "Damn," she finally said, wiping her eyes and disappearing back into the classroom.

An hour of the school day remained, so I went into the classroom and called for everyone's attention. "I'm sure you kids have worn Mrs. Jones to a frazzle today," I said, "so everyone who thinks she deserves a rest while the rest of us go down to the creek and tell some stories raise their hands."

It was, as always, unanimous.

The razor-edged bits of winter soon began to close in on the Trans-Pecos, its cold winds freezing out the sun's warmth by day and causing desperate searchings for long stored blankets at night. For many it is the hardest of times in Terlingua.

Rarely a day would pass when at some point Mayberry's evaluation didn't come to rest its weight on my shoulders. Regardless of how many times I told myself to toss away the negative feelings he had draped over our situation and continue the effort to set things right, depression succeeded in sneaking up on me.

"If the people around here see the slightest indication that you're about ready to throw in the towel," Olga had warned, "they'll sit down and give up before you know what's happened. They're watching you. You're the gauge they're reading every day. If you're on top of things, they're convinced that progress is going ahead. Mope around, and I'll bet you I can go down to the post office and hear a half dozen rumors about the fact the school's going to be shut down."

I had carefully explained to the members of the school board the things Mayberry had discussed with me, stopping short of making them aware that he had left me with the impression that what we were trying to do fell well within his definition of impossibility. I figured that if people are to try to accomplish the impossible, their chances of success are enhanced if they are not aware of their task's impossibility. Still, I had tried to provide them with an honest report at the most recent school board meeting, outlining the lengthy list of shortcomings the Texas Education Agency continued to find in our operation.

Daisy Adams had accepted the latest report passively. In her years in Terlingua, she had often pointed out to me, she couldn't recall the number of times she had heard that the school was going to be closed for one reason or another. To her, this was just another chapter in an old story.

"I've been able to look out and see kids playing on this very school ground since nineteen forty-four," she said. "Even when I try, I can't really imagine there being no school.

"You know," she continued, "rules are good. I believe in them. The country couldn't survive without them. But the older I get, the more I wonder if the same set of rules ought to be applied to everyone, with no exception, like your Mr. Mayberry says. The fact is, those folks in Austin don't have the slightest idea what life is like out here. In more than a few ways, this is still frontier country. People out here sometimes get so busy just trying to keep body and soul together that they don't have time to stop and think much about what rules they might be breaking."

In the years I've been here, a steady stream of people have come to the area, determined to make a new, less complicated life for themselves, only to be soundly defeated by the land and the life-style it dictates. I've seen great displays of enthusiasm erode to wearied defeat and watched as people proudly, angrily, hung on until the last bit of hope was spent before packing their belongings and moving away.

I have, in fact, come to a point where I am just as skeptical of newcomers' chances as residents were of mine four years ago.

Only this week I had found Matt Simmons sitting soberly at

his desk while the other students were outside for noon recess. "You feeling bad?" I asked.

"No."

"Then what's the matter?"

Big tears welled in his eyes. "Carlos had to move away," he answered.

I had noticed the empty desks normally occupied by Carlos Villa, Matt's best friend, and Carlos's sister Alma, and had assumed their absence was because of sickness or their father's need for them to help with some job Matt's father might have at the Lajitas Trading Post. Such was not the case. There simply had not been enough work to provide the Villa family a living and they had moved in search of a more prosperous place to call home.

Theirs is not an unusual story. Lured here by promises of cheap land and peace and quiet, people withdraw their savings from the bank and arrive convinced that the wildest of vocational plans will work.

Several summers ago a widowed mother and her young daughter bought a small place out in the desert, hired a couple of wetbacks to build them a temporary home that was little more than a shack, and advised those who inquired that they planned to raise rabbits for a living. Plans for the home they would eventually build, she said, were already being drawn up.

Except to bring her daughter to school, the mother was seldom seen in town, and on more than one occasion I wondered where she was marketing the rabbits she was raising. My concern grew early that winter when the girl was absent for several days. Finally I suggested to Olga that, if the girl was not in school soon, she drive out to their place to see if everything was okay.

That evening, however, a knock came at the door. It was the little girl. She had walked to our house, the fifteen-mile trip taking her most of the day, and she was exhausted. Her mother, she said, was sick. Could we come see about her?

Leaving her with Olga, I drove the pickup across the all but impassable road to their house. There were no lights, nor was there any answer to my calls and knocks. Letting myself in, I found the woman on a pallet in the corner, covered with blankets in an attempt to shield herself from the bitter cold of the unheated room. No doctor's trained eye was necessary to see that she was suffering from advanced stages of pneumonia. As I lifted her and carried her to the pickup, I realized that her condition was no doubt complicated considerably by malnutrition.

Unlike the Villas, she had not known when to give up.

I made a quick stop by the house to tell Olga I was taking the child's mother to the hospital in Alpine and would probably be late getting home.

While her mother recuperated, the girl remained with us. The day after my trip to Alpine I drove her out to her house so she could pick up some clothes and her schoolbooks. As she gathered her things inside, I walked around the house outside and found a row of empty rabbit hutches, doors hanging open, feed bowls long empty.

Driving back toward the school I asked her, "What happened to all your rabbits?"

She did not take her eyes off the road, looking straight ahead in an attempt to avoid the embarrassment I was immediately sorry to have caused her. "We ate them," she said.

After her mother was released from the hospital she checked her daughter out of school and left.

Their home no longer sits on the land they once so eagerly settled on. It has long since been moved to a nearby ranch where it is now being used for a chicken coop.

$\mathcal{VI}$

Perhaps our generation will come to appreciate [the Southwest] as the country God remembered and saved for man's delight when he could mature enough to understand it. God armored it ... with thorns on the trees, stings and horns on the bugs and beasts. He fortified it with mountain ranges and trackless deserts. He filled it with such hazards as no legendary hero ever had to surmount... .

—from Our Southwest by Erna Fergusson

Bob Burton, with his crew-cut hairstyle, his cheeky red face, and his stocky, muscular build, looks every bit the aging high-school football coach he once was. Settling onto one of the yellow vinyl stools at the Study Butte Cafe and ordering a Budweiser, he also looked tired, weary of driving the endless miles that were now behind him. He pulled off the blue stocking cap he was wearing and rolled up the sleeves of his plaid flannel shirt. On each arm was a tattoo.

"Haven't seen you around for a while," Willa Ranallo said as she popped the top of the can of beer she had retrieved from the icebox. "Country's going to hell and can't nobody find you. Way I see it, you got a lotta work cut out for you this time around."

Burton exploded into a rumbling laugh. "Fella ran into my trailer in Alpine a while back," he explained, "and I've had it in the shop. Got her fixed up now, though, and I'm back on the road, so the devil better start watching his step." Now it was Willa's turn to laugh.

"We're having services up at the schoolhouse tonight," Burton said, setting his Budweiser down after taking a long drink from it. "You gonna be able to make it?"

"I will if I can get somebody to tend this place," she said. "We'd be glad to have you," Burton said. "But if you can't get away you oughta send the kids. The wife's got some crafts and things planned for the young ones."

Burton, forty-nine, is the Episcopal archdeacon of the Trans-Pecos, a sort of modern-day circuit-riding preacher who brings religion to the Terlingua area once a month in a trailer home he pulls behind his pickup. He had earlier unhitched the trailer down the highway at the school grounds, leaving his wife to make things ready for the evening worship service while he visited around, letting people know he was in town.

His mission accomplished at the cafe, he walked back out to his dust-covered pickup, stopping long enough to chat a moment with a couple of ranchers who had just driven up and invited them to the services, then drove off to call on the handful of faithfuls he knew who would help him to make residents aware of his arrival.

"Gonna be a fine meeting tonight," he said. "We've got some new songbooks to pass out. Yessir, we'll make a joyful noise, I'll guarantee you that."

The Burtons live in Van Horn where they work with a small Episcopal congregation when they aren't on the road serving the tiny missions in such outposts as Marfa, Alpine, Pecos, and Fort Stockton. In addition to Terlingua they also pay regular visits to small groups who worship in his trailer church in Sanderson, Balmorhea, Presidio, and Fort Davis. Burton hopes to eventually establish churches in each of the hamlets which would be directed by local people training to become priests. Thus far he has met with little success, but he isn't discouraged.

"For now," he says, "we'll just have to keep hauling this trailer around. I don't mind it. In fact, this trailer of ours ties the whole area together. You hear people saying all the time, 'Sure, I'd love to come to church, but it's too far.' So we just tell 'em, 'Don't worry about that; we'll bring the church to you.' The apostle Paul also traveled quite a few miles establishing churches, you know."

It is doubtful, however, that Paul covered the ground Burton does. The diocese he serves is roughly the size of New England – 30,000 square miles, but the area is inhabited by only 45,000 people. Back in Cleveland, Ohio, where Bob and Phyllis did lay work for the city's oldest Episcopal church, there were 10,000 people within a square mile of the church. Out here there are one and one-half people per square mile.

By strict religious standards Bob Burton is not a prototype of what a man of God is supposed to be. His approach is low-keyed with a welcome absence of fire and brimstone. He is a Christian by action rather than word.

"People out in this part of the world fight a daily battle to survive. It's hard work that can get to be pretty discouraging at times. They aren't going to come to our services to be reprimanded for their sins. They're looking for hope and a little comfort."

As a result, Bob spends a lot more time just chatting with

people, hoping to get to know them a little better and allow them to get to know him, than he does conducting church services.

While Burton is making some inroads, progress is slow. There are many residents of the Terlingua area who have made it clear that they have neither time nor need for religion. If as many as twenty people cram themselves into the trailer-church for his service, Bob is pleased.

For myself it is a matter of priorities. Olga, after having coffee with Phyllis Burton earlier in the afternoon, was looking forward to the evening service. I generally worried more about the plumbing than about my eternal soul. That night, for example, I was lying on my back on the kitchen floor, my head inside the cabinet beneath the sink, muttering a few things that would hardly please the visiting church official. As I worked, tools scattered about on the kitchen floor and water soaking everything in sight, Olga sat at the kitchen table applying gentle persuasion to try to get me to say I'd attend Burton's service.

Over in the trailer Phyllis completed her routine of cleaning up and Bob set up a small altar complete with candles, silver chalice, and white cloth. He changed into his black shirt and clerical collar but decided against wearing the white and gold vestments that hung in the closet. "That's one good thing about this type ministry," he often said. "Folks out here don't exactly stand on formality. They're lucky in that respect. They don't feel any great need for it. They take a man for what he is and don't pay much attention to anything else. That, to me, is one of the greatest of Christian principles."

Back in the Jones house Olga was startled by a sudden yell from beneath the kitchen sink. "Get out the champagne," I cried. "Let's celebrate."

"Did you get it fixed?" Olga asked.

"Nope," I replied, "but I got it down to just one little drip."

"Maybe," Olga suggested, "you ought to come to church with me and give thanks for that."

I began to laugh as I picked up my tools. "Maybe I should at that."

A calm darkness had descended over the desert, broken only by the display of stars and the headlights of occasional cars and pickups coming down the dirt road to the Burtons' trailer. By 7:30, eighteen people, mostly women and their children, were seated in the folding chairs crowded into the tiny church on wheels.

Standing over the makeshift altar, Burton looked even larger than before. His voice was warm, welcoming, and resonant with an unmistakable mid-western accent. "I consider myself an institutional church member who sees Christianity not as a bolt of lightning that hits you out of the blue but as the work we do day by day."

His sermon was brief, accented by several hymns led by his wife. Olga played her guitar as Irene Ranallo, clearly the best singer in the congregation, led the youngsters in attendance in the singing of "Everything Is Beautiful." Burton then offered communion to anyone who wished to partake. "The body of

Christ, the bread of heaven," he repeated as he gently made his way between the chairs to each person. The service ended with a prayer and the gathering immediately turned into a social occasion, the adults talking and the children working on their paper cutouts with Phyllis Burton.

"When this type ministry was first approved," Burton told one of the newcomers to his services, "the bishop didn't know what the hell was going on because it had never been tried before. But that's what I like about trying new things — you've got a lot of freedom to experiment because there are no precedents, no rules to get tangled up in."

That philosophy, perhaps better than anything else, enables Bob Burton to fit into the world of the Trans-Pecos. That freedom he speaks of is something virtually every resident of the area values, indeed one of the primary reasons they are here.

The following morning Burton was up early, saying hello to several of the parents as they arrived at the school with their children, then was off to visit several homes. His wife, her pet poodle, Buffy, in tow, had caught a ride out to visit Irene, who was in town for a visit.

The Burtons, after a year of visits, have gotten closer to some of the people of Terlingua, gaining their confidence and respect. Still, there is no indication that anyone is interested in taking on the pastoral duties of the community. In Marfa, the editor of the weekly newspaper showed interest in studying for the priesthood. In Van Horn, a wool broker indicated he would like to establish a church. In Terlingua, however, Burton has found no takers.

"The funding for this project," he told me, "was set up for a three-year period. It was felt that in that period of time we should be able to establish local churches and have the respective communities working on their own. I don't know what happens when the gas money runs out."

Until it does, he will continue to make his monthly pilgrimages to Terlingua, making friends, spreading the gospel, and carrying on his search for someone to continue his work.

"Patience is more than a virtue in this part of the country," he says. "It's a tool of survival. You just keep hoping something will happen and, if you're lucky, it will. Maybe next month someone will come forward."

None of the Ernie Harmon family ever attends Brother Bob's (as the people of Terlingua call him) services. A self proclaimed Baptist missionary and one-time carpet layer who abandoned his career in hopes of establishing a Mexican mission in the Trans-Pecos, Harmon insists that he and members of his family are Fundamentalists who observe a more strict religious doctrine than that served up by Burton from his chapel on wheels. Instead, Harmon offers residents of Terlingua their only religious alternative: Thursday evening Bible Study classes which he conducts at the school.

Though one of his most faithful attendants, Olga is quite often a painful, frustrating thorn in Harmon's side. The cousin of a Greek Orthodox priest, my wife is better versed than most in a variety of religious philosophies and is not the least hesitant to challenge Harmon on points he seeks to drive home on Thursday evenings.

The Harmon children, on the other hand — Brian, a sixth grader; Stephanie, a third-grader; and Barbara who is in the first — live by a strict set of rules which they daily brought to school with them. The girls, for instance, are not allowed to wear anything but dresses, can't participate in any kind of activity that involves dancing, and would not, on strict orders from their parents, sing any songs that aren't patriotic or religious in nature. Brian, whose hair is cut shorter than most of the other boys in school, refers to many of his male classmates as "hippies."

The Harmon children had enrolled in the fall after having taken a correspondence curriculum the year before. Mr. Harmon came to me and asked about enrolling his children; I told him we would be happy to have them. He said that he understood that we had a pretty large enrollment already and if the addition of his three kids would create a problem he would just order the correspondence courses again.

One more year of correspondence courses, isolated from the rest of the Terlingua children, I felt, and the Harmon children might become lost causes.

Despite the restrictions placed on their young lives at virtually every turn, all three had quickly adapted to their new academic environment. Only in the first few weeks of school did Olga and I worry about our new students.

Sitting in the kitchen one evening after dinner, I began to smile. "Olga," I asked, "have you ever seen anyone enjoy a candy bar more than Brian Harmon? The only time he really lets himself go and acts like a kid is when he's chomping on a candy bar. Damn, he savors every bite, like it's a religious experience in itself."

"Like father, like son," Olga said, smiling, as she washed dishes. It was something of a community joke that if the Chevron station ran out of Milky Ways, Ernie Harmon just might be forced to give up his mission work and return to carpet laying in a more civilized environment. Already overweight, a man who walked with a jarring, heavy step, Harmon's daily routine seldom varied. Each day, generally at midmorning, he would appear at the station, ponder the contents of the candy counter for several seconds, and finally repeat the same words he had said the day before: "I guess," he would say, as if relieved of a heavy decision, "I'll have one of those Milky Ways."

When his son had first arrived at school he was withdrawn and spoke to hardly anyone, even his sisters. When he would be among the last chosen to participate in the games at recess or during physical education class, his attitude would become defensive and he would retreat back into the classroom and begin reading a book.

In those first weeks Olga repeatedly expressed her concern about Brian to me. "Don't worry about him," I would say, "Brian's a smart kid. Just give him a little time. Pretty soon he'll realize that he's got to take the first step himself. He wants to play, to be a part of things, badly enough to figure out how to get involved. We'll just let him learn what he has to do."

Before long Brian was totally involved in all the activities of the school. All, that is, except for the one many of the students held to be the most enjoyable of each day.

After lunch I would place a videotape of "The Electric Company" on the television set in back of the room and allow the students to watch it before returning to classroom activities. "Mr. Jones," he had said, "momma and daddy said we couldn't watch 'The Electric Company' if it had any dancing on it." Then, asking a question whose answer he dreaded to hear, he said, "Does it have dancing?"

Well aware that the Harmon definition of dancing included anything that wasn't clearly walking, running, or sitting in a chair, I told Brian that, yes, it did have some. His face fell and without any further conversation he went out onto the playground with his sisters to endure until the corruption of educational television was finished for the day and classes could resume.

For several days I wrestled with the problem, watching each day at noon as the Harmon children finished their sack lunches and then quietly excused themselves to the playground or another part of the room while the rest of the children gathered excitedly around the television set. Already I had been through one mild confrontation with the children's parents about the evils of dance — that coming after Stephanie had told her father that they had done the "twist" in physical education.

Olga, who usually led the children in their exercises, tried to explain to Ernie Harmon that it was nothing more than a calisthenic which involved the rotation of the hips and moving of the arms, but to no avail. "Nonetheless," he had said, unbending, "it seems to involve all the mechanics of some of the modern dancing that young people do today. I would consider it a personal favor if you would allow my children to be dismissed from that particular activity." Olga, calling on great reserves of control, agreed to excuse the Harmon children from all forms of exercise that might be construed as dancing.

After relating her conversation to me in a far less calm manner than she had used in her discussion with Harmon, we decided that it was simply a state of affairs we would have to live with — or step around as delicately as possible. The following day as I loaded the tape into the machine for the noonday viewing of the TV show, Brian, Stephanie, and Barbara began to go outside.

"Wait a minute," I said. "You kids come back here and sit down."

Surprised and obviously excited, the Harmon children took their places in the semicircle in front of the TV set.

"Now," I said, "every once in a while the people on this show do some little dances. Some people think it is okay to dance; others don't. That's fine. What we will do is this: If it looks as if there is going to be some dancing on the show, anyone who isn't supposed to watch it can simply get up and go outside until the dancing is over. When it's over we'll call you, and you can come back in and watch the rest of the show. Does everyone understand?"

At the far edge of the semicircle, the Harmon children, their eyes fixed on the still blank TV screen in anticipation, nodded.

Occasionally Ernie Harmon would stop by the school late in the afternoon to say hello to us and express his pleasure at the academic progress his children were making. They seemed quite happy, he would say, and their grades seemed to indicate that they were doing well in their studies.

I always had sincere praise for the Harmon children, for in truth they were all very good students. Brian, in fact, was doing advanced work and progressing at a rate that at times surprised even me. He loved to read and had displayed a vivid imagination in the stories he had been writing in class. Stephanie, the quietest and shyest of the three, at one time content to let her younger sister serve as her spokeswoman, had begun to open up and participate more freely in class discussions. And Barbara, who had cried that first day when Donna Harmon left her at school, had needed precious little time to develop into one of the most outgoing students. Too young to feel the weight of religious restrictions whose impact on her life she had not yet grasped, she was charmingly mischievous and gifted with a warm sense of humor.

"They're doing quite well, all of them," I told their father. "It pleases me to hear that," Ernie Harmon said. "To be quite honest with you, I was concerned about how they would handle being in school in a mixed-race situation. You just never know how kids are going to react."

The observation came as a surprise to me, particularly from a man whose new calling in life was supposed to be to establish missions for Mexican-Americans.

Harmon, however, obviously saw no irony in his remark and in fact went on to say, "I have made every effort to teach my kids to love all races as I do, to understand that all of us — white people, Mexicans, and niggers — are God's people."

I bit my lip to suppress the laughter building in my throat. Not looking at Harmon for fear that my amusement might reveal itself, I directed my gaze across the school grounds, out toward the distant mountains, and simply nodded. Ernie Harmon accepted that as approval.

As the school year progressed, I learned to adopt a teacher's patience toward the boundaries that Ernie and Donna Harmon placed about their children. Brian, Stephanie, and Barbara were quick, eager learners and, except for those occasions when they sat down to watch while the rest of the group participated in a song or dance, were seldom a problem.

On occasion, however, the teachings the Harmon children were receiving at home would find their way into the curriculum. One morning I noticed small slips of paper being passed around and asked one of the children to show me what she was reading. Printed in pencil, in the hand of a grade-school student, was the following message:

Pray this Prayer. Get saved today. Don't laugh at it.

Dear Lord Jeuse come into my heart save me foregive me with all my sin's. I know I'm a durty rotten siner amene.

I read the prayer, asked that any other copies be handed to the front of the room, and instructed the class not to pass any more notes. Looking at the piece of paper again, I smiled. "We all might be sinners," I could not resist saying" "but I hardly think we're all dirty and rotten."

The students, Stephanie included, laughed and another crisis had passed.

VII

I handed a clipping from the Alpine paper to Olga and said, "Look at this. George Acosta placed second in tool identification and fourth in arc welding, and his brother Larry won first place in vertical fillet welding in an industrial training contest in Abilene." Olga managed a puzzled smile. "I'm glad," she said, "but what does that all mean?" "It means," I replied, "that they're both learning a trade."

Little Gabriel Acosta had come to school for the first time last year as a five-year-old, unable to speak a word of English. Under Texas law any non-English-speaking student can begin the first grade at age five, thus by the time he reported for the second grade Gabriel's English had improved greatly.

Still, we were not without our communication breakdowns from time to time.

Someone had accidentally locked the door to the bathroom, and since there was no key it was decided that Gabriel, because he was by far the smallest of all the students, would be lifted through the small window outside into the bathroom so that he might unlock the door. Once inside, however, it became apparent that he had not completely understood his mission. Rather than unlock the door, he flushed the toilet. "It works good, Mr. Jones," he yelled through the door. "Nothing wrong. See?" He flushed it again.

Laughter immediately erupted among the students. Gabriel's sister Iselda, frustrated and somewhat embarrassed by her younger brother's failure to carry out his task, quickly stepped to the door and in biting Spanish informed him to quit flushing the toilet and unlock the door. In a few seconds Gabriel opened the door and sheepishly peeked out. Aware that his sister was not altogether pleased with his performance, he avoided her tight-jawed look and instead focused on me. "Everything's okay, Mr. Jones," he said.

"Good, Gabriel," I said, "You've been a big help."

Despite such occasional misunderstandings, Gabriel has made tremendous progress. Last year when he was a first grader, I did nothing but work with him on English, slowly teaching him words, then phrases, and finally sentences. By the end of the school year he was taking books home which he would read over and over before returning them. Generally, it takes about two years for the Spanish-speaking children to make the transition to English well enough to begin making headway in other subjects, but Gabriel's progress has been such that I'm sure he'll be able to begin doing some math and science this year.

Of all the families I've met since coming to Terlingua, the Acostas, lifelong residents of this region, are the ones I most admire. Hilario Acosta, the father, can neither speak, read, nor write English and earns his living doing a variety of odd jobs for the ranchers and the local highway department until school is out each spring. He then takes the entire family north to join a force of migrant field workers for the summer. Insistent, however, that his five children get the education he never received, he always has them back in Terlingua in time for the first day of school.

His wife, Dominga, a short heavy-set woman who seems always to be in high spirits, maintains a vegetable garden, a small herd of goats, milks a cow twice daily, and feeds and cares for her family off the land in a manner that Euell Gibbons would no doubt have admired and probably been amazed at. Dominga taught Olga how to make a delicious goat's milk cheese called asadero using the juice of trompillo berries — which are generally considered to be poisonous — instead of the standard rennet. The cabrito she barbecues after her husband has butchered one of the young goats is outstanding.

Her talents as a gardener and jelly maker (from native cactus fruits) are supplemented by the hunting abilities of Hilario and her sons. Canned goods, in fact, are seldom to be found in the small pantry Mrs. Acosta keeps in one end of their house trailer.

The Acostas' ability to live almost totally off a land that many look upon as virtually unyielding is a constant source of amazement to me. But it is not accomplished without a constant and concerted group effort that involves every member of the family, right down to six-year-old Gabriel.

The boys purchase most of their own school clothes with money earned each year by trapping fox, coyote, and raccoon and selling the pelts to a traveling fur trader who makes periodic stops at their home. They help their father haul water to the dry patch of land they lease near Study Butte and they till their mother's garden without benefit of any of the modern-day gardening conveniences Mrs. Acosta occasionally stops in to admire in the Sears catalogue down at the post office. Iselda helps with the housework and the weekly washing, which is done on an old wringer-type machine, and shares kitchen responsibilities with her mother.

They are a proud family who, despite the hardships of life in Terlingua, has chosen it as their home rather than the Santa Elena village across the river in Mexico where many of their relatives still live. Occasionally they go there for a visit, driving their old pickup to the river, taking a boat across, and walking the remainder of the way to the tiny community of adobe huts. They never go without gifts, generally clothing collected by the traveling Brother Bob who makes regular stops in Terlingua for monthly services.

The two oldest Acosta boys, George and Larry, have graduated from the Terlingua School and now ride the bus daily to school in Alpine. Five days a week they are up at four in the morning so they can accomplish a few predawn chores before their father drives them the twenty miles up the highway to the bus stop. Precious little daylight remains by the time they arrive back home, thus most of the chores they are responsible for are done on the weekends.

It is a schedule few teenagers would find palatable. But despite the grueling routine, the older Acosta boys have done well. Teachers, you should know, are constantly looking for students whom they can point to as proof that their programs are indeed succeeding. George and Larry are two of my best arguments whenever I hear the comment that students attending small schools encounter great difficulty when they are forced to move into larger, more sophisticated school systems. Their grades in Alpine – which they keep me posted about – are well above average. George, in fact, is regularly on the honor roll. I rest my case.

I'm sure the three Acostas who are still in Terlingua School will do just as well when time comes for them to transfer to Alpine. Iselda, who is twelve, is an exceptionally bright student. A lovely girl who is always seeking beauty hints from Olga, she has been a tremendous help to me since I came here. As something of a self-appointed mother hen to the younger students, she often watches the younger children for me during physical education period, and it is Iselda who generally takes on the responsibility of orienting any new students. Her help with the Mexican-American students with little knowledge of English has been invaluable. She also has a beautiful singing voice and learned to play the guitar from Olga. When I finally managed to repair an old sewing machine I'd found stored shortly after my arrival here and began trying to afford the girls a little homemaking experience, Iselda moved quickly to the head of the class although she was only nine at the time.

Her brother Richard, a year younger than she, was by far the shyest of the Acosta children and faced the greatest difficulty with the language problem when he began school. He was a second grader my first year here and I was puzzled that his sister and brothers seemed to enjoy school while he made no visible effort to even try to like it.

After a few weeks, I went to Mrs. Acosta to talk to her about

Richard. "School embarrasses him," she said. "Last year he did very poorly. He learned very little, I'm afraid, and the teacher told him he was never going to be a very good pupil. This year he cried when it came time to return to school. He begged me to let him stay home and help around the house. He said he had forgotten everything he had learned the first year. My heart aches for him, Mr. Jones. He sees the other children doing well and enjoying school and he knows he is standing alone. He needs encouragement. I try to give it to him, but I am not a smart person. I do not know much about books and lessons. The older children try to help him, but they become frustrated with him and they have their own lessons to do. I will help in any way you suggest, but also I would ask that you try to do what you can to help Richard. He's a good boy."

I immediately began spending more time with Richard. I seized on the slightest opportunity to praise him. I made him aware that if he worked hard he could be a good student. I struck a deal with him: I told him that if he would try as hard as he could for a few months, I would do the same and the end result would be that he would begin to learn and enjoy school.

I also enlisted the help of his sister and brothers. They agreed to help Richard with his lessons — particularly his reading — at home in the evenings.

Slowly at first, and then with a pace that even surprised me, Richard began to improve. And with that improvement came the confidence that had not been there before. Richard began to smile, to participate in the discussions and the outdoor activities.

Though still a quiet youngster, he was no longer embarrassed about his academic progress. In the fifth grade this year, he is one of my most studious pupils and maintains a straight-A report card.

When the questionnaires were passed out to all the parents prior to the showdown school board meeting last year, Mrs. Acosta wrote in great detail of Richard's progress, giving me more credit than I deserved.

One afternoon when most of the students had already left for the day, Iselda remained behind to help clean the blackboards. A girl who has inherited her mother's constant cheerfulness, she talked nonstop about the things we were doing at school. "Mr. Jones," she said as she gathered up her books in preparation for the short walk home, "this school is just a part of my family. I love it. Someday, after I have gone to college and learned the things I need to learn, I want to be a teacher. Maybe by then you won't want to teach anymore and I can become the teacher here."

"Iselda," I said, "I can't think of anyone I would rather turn my job over to than you. You just keep working hard and maybe one day all that will happen."

She smiled, satisfied, and left for home. Later, when I recounted the conversation to Olga, she laughed. "Well, Mr. Jones," she said, "I have this to say for you. You had best not become too lax in your duties since there is now someone who has publicly admitted she's after your job. I suggest you bear down."

The truth of the matter is that I had been bearing down, and then some, since the school board turmoil had finally quieted and the focus of attention had finally returned to the problem of meeting the accreditation requirements. From the day school opened, I seemed to be constantly meeting myself coming and going. For the eight grades I taught, there were a total of fifty-three different textbooks used, and the large number of students made my Sunday routine of preparing lesson plans even more difficult. I tried nevertheless to plan each school day in a way that would still allow me time to deal with each student individually as much as possible.

Managing a classroom of only twelve or fifteen students had not been that difficult. I would, for instance, get the first-graders busy drawing a picture or looking at a book and tell them not to ask any questions for fifteen minutes. I would then proceed on to the next grade, get it started on an assignment and tell them, too, that it would be fifteen minutes before I could deal with any of their questions. By the time I had gone through the eight grades, it would be time to make the rounds again, answering questions, engaging in group discussions, and giving personal attention to individual problems.

The cycle process was still workable, but the amount of time I was able to give to each individual seemed to get shorter and shorter. From 8:45 A.M. to 3:45 P.M. there just never seemed to be enough time.

Olga, who earned her degree in speech and drama at Trinity University, had agreed to come to work as an unofficial and unpaid part-time aide, leaving Cassandra with Mrs. Acosta for a few hours and bringing Anna to class each day. The children enjoyed her, and her regular presence helped take some of the load off me. The presence of a qualified aide had also been one of the TEA's requirements for a group of our size and grade range, so I hoped the new school board would eventually formalize the arrangement. As soon as the new school board members had been sworn in, they'd asked me to begin research on the things that had to be done to meet the accreditation requirements. They would, in turn, begin looking into the proper procedure for having the taxable land in the school district reevaluated so that the existing tax structure could be revised. Thus while letters were being written to taxpayers, explaining to them the Texas Education Agency's demands, and a meeting was being scheduled with a tax collector to see when a vote on the issue might be held, I pondered the forms that would have to be filled out, the need for expanding our new building, and spent several summer days in the Sul Ross University library in Alpine researching curriculum guides.

Of all the tasks facing us, the preparation of those guides seemed to be the most demanding. They had to include a detailed outline of how each subject in each grade would be taught. Wording would have to be exact, and details were endless. I checked around and found that virtually all schools, large and small, hired professional academic experts to write the guides for them. The fee, I was told, generally ran in the $12,000 range. It might as well have been $12 million so far as the Terlingua School was concerned.

I talked to Glenn Pepper. "Glenn," I said, "there's no way I can do those things and teach too. I'm not sure I could do them even if they were all I had to do. A New York lawyer would have trouble. They're complicated as hell with a lot of wording that would make a college professor go to the dictionary. We've got to hire someone to do them or everything else we do will be a big waste of time."

Glenn pointed out that Judge Thomas had indicated to him that there might be some funds available for such a project. "I didn't get the impression," he said, "that there would be anywhere near that much available, though."

"Hell," I said, frustrated, "I don't think there's that much money in all of Brewster County."

Later it occurred to me that the small school in neighboring Big Bend National Park must be facing the same need, so I drove up there to talk with the school board president. The school, attended by children of employees in the park, was not as financially strapped as we were, yet the prospect of paying out thousands of dollars for a set of curriculum guides had not been greeted with open arms there either. Since we both needed basically the same set of guides, I proposed we split the expense of having them written. After several discussions, the park officials agreed. A second stroke of luck came about when Daisy Adams's sister, Elvie Williams, suggested a retired Sul Ross professor still living in Alpine who might be willing to take on the job for a reasonable fee.

By the end of the summer the first full-fledged miracle I've ever been witness to took place. Dr. Raymond Wheat, a kindly gentleman with time on his hands since his teaching career had ended, agreed to prepare the twenty-seven volumes that would meet the curriculum-guide needs of both Terlingua and the Big Bend school. It was Daisy who brought the good news.

"My sister," she said, "must have laid it on pretty thick, telling him how the state was bound and determined to shut us down and how we didn't have much money and all. He's going to do whatever it is you need for a couple of thousand. I've talked with Glenn and he tells me we shouldn't have too much trouble raising our half of that. What do you think?"

I was speechless. "Daisy," I finally said, "what I think is, if we are able to pull this whole accreditation thing off and keep this school going, some kind of monument should be erected to Dr. Wheat right out on the school grounds."

Thus as the school year began I found comfort in the fact that at least one phase of the program was under way. Dr. Wheat had said he would have the guides completed, before the end of the school year. That would just beat the TEA's deadline.

In the meantime I spent evenings with questionnaires and forms spread across the kitchen table. Each had to be completed and returned to various government agencies as well as the accreditation board. There were, for example, things like the Elementary and Secondary School Civil Rights Survey circulated by the Department of Health, Education and Welfare. It contained twelve pages of questions, and six copies were needed. In the section seeking information on the ethnic makeup of our school, the categories included Alaskan natives, Hispanics, American Indians, and Chinese. They also wanted to know if our non-existent toilet stalls were wide enough to accommodate wheelchairs; how many elevators were in our building; what educational opportunities were available for minority students; and how our school buses were maintained.

The truth of the matter was, I found myself looking hard for questions that applied to our school. I cursed the absurdity of it all and kept filling in the blanks, generally with the phrase "Does not apply."

One evening Pam Gaddis, a friend who lived over near the post office, came by while I was filling out forms and looked over my shoulder. "Oh-oh," she said. "I never thought of anything like that. Seems to me if you have any hopes of getting your school accredited you're going to have to begin building at least one elevator for it right away."

"Yeah," said Olga, "and we're going to have to scrounge up a native Alaskan willing to enroll in a little desert school soon, too."

I couldn't help but laugh with them.

A few days later Pam stopped by the school and stuck her head in the door. I was in the middle of class, but she motioned me over with great urgency. "Here's a little present," she said, "that will be invaluable to you when you have some more of those forms to fill out." Before I could reply, she turned and left, pedaling away on her multicolored bicycle that the children love to ride.

Later in the day, as the time neared for lunch, I opened the package she had brought, stared at it for a moment, and broke into uncontrolled laughter which had several of the students wondering if perhaps the teacher had finally reached the end of his sanity.

"What's so funny, Mr. Jones?" David Thrift asked, peering over at my gift through his oversize horn-rimmed glasses.

"Oh, it's just a little nutty present Pam brought by," I explained.

What she had given me was a rubber stamp and ink pad, which the accompanying note explained, would save me considerable amounts of writing. The word on the stamp, printed in large capital letters, was "BALONEY."

In days to come, as the paper work seemed to have no end, there was a great temptation to put Pam's stamp to use. But since there had been no hint of a sense of humor in the correspondence I had received from the Texas Education Agency advising me that a member of its auditing and accreditation board would soon be arriving to inspect our progress, I continued to plow through the questions in a businesslike manner. I would eventually come to the decision that the word on Pam's stamp was not really the one I was looking for anyway.

One evening, as I toiled over a form seeking information about our accident-prevention program, Olga returned from having to put the children to bed and sat down across the table from me. "Trent," she said firmly, "I know this is not easy for you and that a lot of what you're having to do is senseless, but if I hear you yell 'bullshit' one more time while Anna and Cassandra are where they can hear you, I'm going to hit you over the head with the broom."

Guilty as charged, I apologized.

At Olga's urging I put the forms away for the night while she went to the icebox for a couple of beers. I went in to check on the girls who were already sleeping, knotted into their impossible postures of slumber. One pillow had already found its way onto the floor and had been quickly claimed by Samantha, the little Dalmatian Olga had christened Sam as a pup only to learn later that the name did not properly match the dog's gender.

I stood looking down at the girls for several minutes, my presence disturbing only the family pet who opened her eyes and lifted her head ever so slightly. Once satisfied that I was not there to banish her from her pillow bed, she sighed and went back to sleep.

The kids love it here, I thought to myself. Since she'd started coming to school with Olga, Anna had been adopted as the unofficial class mascot and the students saw to it that she was allowed to participate in the recess games with some of the younger children. She was already eager for another year to pass so that she, too, might join the first graders in their daily class work. Cassandra, now almost two, was the only native of Terlingua in the family. I've never known of a more happy baby.

I knew that much of what I was doing here was for personal, even selfish, motives. It was a life-style I had dreamed of and had finally found. But it was also for these two little girls. One day — too soon probably — they would grow up and set courses of their own. By that time progress would have dealt a lethal blow to the Terlinguas of the country, but I was firmly convinced that, no matter what their future held, the experience of growing up here, in a simpler place and time, would provide them an advantage few their age would have ever gained. To spend their formative academic years in a small school, molded and guided by a teacher who has time to encourage them and teach them, was, I believed, the best gift I could give them.

They too, then, were part of the reason I was filling out forms and building additional shelving and engaging in an almost constant preoccupation with improvement of the school before the accreditation inspector's decision.

Tacked on the wall above her bed was a picture Anna had colored in school the day before. It was a picture of the sun shining brightly on a field of what she later informed me was supposed to be corn. The stalks were enormous and laden with giant ears of bright yellow corn. Even the most prosperous farmer in Iowa would have had difficulty believing such a bountiful crop. And here, in rainless Terlingua, where Mrs. Acosta fights a continuing battle just to keep her tomato plants alive, it was impossible.

I smiled at the picture, then at its artist. Bending over to kiss her, I said, "Keep dreaming, you little dreamer."

Then I went into the kitchen and slowly drank my beer while Olga strummed on her guitar.

I don't know how long I had been sleeping before I sat up in the bed and began shaking Olga awake. "I know," I told her, "where I'm going to get a library."

"At this time of night?" she asked.

Ignoring her semiconscious humor, I rattled off my plan. "You know that prefabricated cabin that the Terremar Corporation was having hauled in, the one that fell off the truck and was damaged so badly? It's been sitting out there on the edge of the highway for weeks now. They haven't made the slightest attempt to do anything with it. They're probably thinking about tearing it up and seeing what lumber they can salvage from it. I'm going to see what they will sell it to us for. I can get some of the men around here to pitch in and I bet we can haul it up here to the school grounds and fix it up just fine. We can put shelves in it and maybe a couple of tables with chairs. It will make a great library. The TEA didn't say anything about the library having to be connected to the main school building."

Now fully awake, Olga added logic to my brainstorm. "Why don't you give the Terremar Corporation the opportunity to donate it to the school? They can write it off that way, I'm sure, and a charitable gesture wouldn't hurt their image any."

The next morning I called Bill McNair, president of the Terremar Corporation, and presented my plan to him. A little surprised that anyone might see the possibility of repairing the structure, he said he would drive down and have another look at the building and get back in touch with me. Two days later he called to say it was in pretty bad shape but it was ours if we wanted it.

"Can it really be made usable?" Olga asked.

"It has to," I told her. "We've got to have additional space and it's lying out there on the side of the road, just waiting. It'll work, Olga. Maybe it won't be something Andrew Carnegie would approve of, but it'll work. We'll fix it up into something the kids will be tickled to death with."

Olga smiled. "You're really just a scavenger at heart aren't you?"

"It goes with the territory," I replied.

Despite the increased enrollment and the added responsibilities of the accreditation paper work, things were going along smoothly as the school year settled into its regular routine. By constantly amending my carefully planned, daily schedules to attend to whatever needs arose, I found I was able to spend more time than I had anticipated working with students on an individual basis.

Gabriel Acosta, as I had hoped, had successfully moved into other areas of study thanks to his improved English and was progressing nicely. Along the way, he was also learning some of the tricks of the student trade. Math not being one of his favored subjects, he devised a rather imaginative plan which worked several times before I finally caught on to what he was doing.

Daily I would write a series of addition and subtraction problems on the board for the younger students to work on, and on several occasions Gabriel would turn in an unfinished paper. "The board was erased before I got finished," he would explain in a sad, trembling voice. "I'll try to go faster tomorrow."

Eventually I learned that after he felt the other second graders had had the proper amount of time to complete the assignment, he would quietly suggest to one of the other children that they ask to be allowed to erase the board for me.

For his ingenuity, I would have to give Gabriel an A. But for his math lessons, the mark would have to be a bit lower.

VIII

I live one day at a time,
I dream one dream at a time... .

— Willie Nelson

Out here, where there is little man-made noise to muffle the sounds of nature, you can hear a storm coming long before it actually hits. It will begin with a soft rumble in the mountains and then graduate to a higher pitch until finally, just before it arrives, it sounds like a train rushing across a long bridge. Before a single drop of moisture has fallen you can hear the water rushing down the canyons and draws as if trying to out race the oncoming clouds. There are no soft, gentle rains in the Trans-Pecos. When they do come it is with a vengeance, as if the clouds, having little use for the desolate region, want to spend as little time as possible at their duty.

I had planned to spend a couple of hours after school had been dismissed welding some of the desks that were in need of repair. Then the rain hit. One minute it had been hot and deathly still; then, as if Mother Nature had flipped a switch, a cool wind swept across the desert and in a matter of seconds a torrential rain was beating down onto the powdered soil. Soaked by the time I had made the fifty-foot run to the house, I entered to find Olga gleefully raising windows and taking the rugs up from the floor and piling them on the bed.

For a moment I said nothing, watching as she hurried about the house barefoot and with her jeans rolled up to the knees. "Mind if I ask what you're doing?"

She gave me a quick glance and smiled as she hurried about her task. "Isn't it wonderful?" she said. "I'm going to let all this clean rainwater blow in so I can give the floors a good mopping. Would you set my plants outside so they can get a drink?"

"It beats talking to them," I replied as I took off my shoes and began walking around the rain-soaked floor gathering pots and hanging baskets.

Such is the welcome the infrequent rains receive in this part of the world.

Before Olga had completed her spur-of-the-moment floor cleaning, the storm was over. The sun reappeared even, before the rivulets of water on the road had stopped running and the temperature quickly climbed back to a degree sufficient to cause steam to rise from the newly moistened ground. With it came a fresh, clean smell I shall not attempt to describe. Suffice it to say it would not be familiar to city dwellers anywhere in the world.

Earlier in the day Donna Pepper had called Olga to invite us over for dinner. Thus as soon as the impromptu cleaning session was done we changed into dry clothes and drove out the highway toward the Peppers' Villa de la Mina, eagerly anticipating the first taste of Donna's Mexican food. Texas Monthly magazine had devoted an entire article to Mexican food in one of its recent issues and mentioned that the food served to river riders who patronize the Peppers' modest resort can expect to find meals "as good as you can find anywhere north of the Rio Bravo."

Though several light-years away from being a qualified gourmet critic, I have absolutely no argument with the magazine's claim.

As we turned off the highway near the ghost town, onto the rocky road leading to the Peppers' house, I stopped the pickup and turned off the motor. Neither Olga nor I spoke. Even the girls were quiet, their giggling silenced as soon as the motor had been shut off.

The most brilliant rainbow I've ever seen arched across the sky, playing on the final rays of sunlight. It appeared to begin over at the base of the Christmas Mountains and end over an area of old abandoned mine shafts just a few hundred yards from where we were parked.

"That," said Olga in a whisper, "is the most beautiful thing I've ever seen. It seems to light the whole sky."

"It looks as if you could walk over the ridge and stand in it," I remarked.

"Let's do, daddy," Anna pleaded. "Let's go stand in the rainbow."

I found myself smiling. "Honey, we could never catch it. Rainbows run away from you. The longer you chase them, the faster they run away. They're just there to be looked at and enjoyed."

Olga looked over at me and took my hand. "For a man who has spent so much time chasing them himself, you put that quite nicely," she said.

When we arrived at the Peppers' they were all sitting on the rock porch watching the colorful show. Donna waved and yelled, "Come on up and join us."

"Pepper," I said as I got out of the pickup, "all your troubles are over. From up on the ridge back down the road we could see the end of the rainbow clear as day. It's right over one of those old mine shafts. My bet is you've got gold down there and didn't even know it."

Glenn Pepper replied, "It'll just have to wait until morning. Donna's got supper ready."

Thirteen years ago Glenn Pepper came to Terlingua to prospect, hoping to find some overlooked vein of mercury that might be mined without a great deal of expensive machinery. Like others before him who had entertained the same hope and the countless numbers who would follow after him, Glenn, called Pepper by everyone who knows him, failed. That failure, however, did little to dim his appreciation for the country. In his six years of rugged, adventuresome existence, searching the land around Perry's old mines, he came to love the region, not to mention a young widow named Donna Thrift whom he had met on his infrequent trips to Alpine for renewal of supplies.

Once satisfied that his prospecting was a lost cause, Pepper began working on another way to remain in the Terlingua area. With the help of a generous bank loan he purchased the old Waldron Mine area, abandoned since 1944, where the shells of several line cabins remained, and set to work on yet another dream. Doing most of the work himself, he remodeled the cabins, bought several rubber rafts, and sought out and trained river travelers to serve as guides on river floats through the towering canyons of the Rio Grande. He also married Donna who eventually assumed the responsibility of seeing to it that the guests would be properly fed during their vacation stays.

The customers came slowly at first and the revenue was barely enough to make ends meet, but as word spread of the Peppers' unique Villa de la Mina (Spanish for Village of the Mines), business increased steadily to a point where he now conducts tours of the mines and float trips through the picturesque canyons the year round. People now come from throughout the Southwest to take advantage of the adventure Pepper's place offers. Politicians, doctors, lawyers, all seeking escape from the gnawing pressures of their jobs, arrive at Villa de la Mina eager to rough it on overnight trips through the Santa Elena or Mariscal or Boquillas canyons.

The Peppers also have something over 1200 Spanish goats roaming their five sections of land. The number fluctuates, depending on the appetites of the cougars, bobcats, and coyotes who also call the ranch home. In recent years, however, the loss of goats has been sharply reduced thanks to four mongrel dogs who as puppies were raised by nannies who had lost their young kids to the elements or the wild animals.

"Those ol' dogs," Pepper explained to me, "are very protective of the herd. They work like a team: Two stand guard around the goats while the other two scout around for any predators roaming nearby. We feed the dogs at night so they bring the goats right up to the pens just before sunset and then lead them back out at daybreak. The truth is, they think they're goats, too."

Indeed they are just as wild. When, in fact, one of the dogs suffers an encounter with a porcupine and returns to the ranch headquarters with the painful quills still stuck in its mouth, Pepper has to rope it to remove the daggers and treat the wounds.

Now as we joined the Peppers on the front porch an old reddish-yellow dog called Rojo, the lead dog of Pepper's guard team, was guiding the last of the goats into the pen where a meal of sotol, chopped earlier by some of Pepper's ranch hands, awaited them.

"Got me a high-class dog coming on," Pepper said, pointing to one of the small pens where a puppy of Catahoula hog dog ancestry was busily nuzzling his dinner from a patient nanny. "One of these days ol' Rojo is going to get too old to stay out all day. It's getting on time to think about training him a replacement."

He motioned me into the house, from which came the inviting smells of tacos and enchiladas. "We'd better try to find us a couple of beers," he said. "If I know Donna, she's made the chili hot enough to burn the bottom out of a cast iron pot."

Clearly Pepper was in a good mood. The surprise rains, which would fill his tanks and give new life to the springs in his canyons, always gave his spirits a lift. In that regard he is no different from any rancher I've ever known. Rain, it might be said, is a tonic that softens facial expressions, erases wrinkles, and brings a new music to the voices of those whose survival is dependent on it.

In addition to his help to me in the capacity of school board president, Glenn Pepper has, since Olga and I arrived here, been our best friend in times of need. Because of his relatively long tenure in this country he has a special understanding of the hardships it offers newcomers, and it was that knowledge, I'm sure, which caused him to be among the first to welcome us to the community with the offer of help anytime it might be needed.

First, it was the loan of the water tank during our first months here. Later there would be even more appreciated gestures. At a time when many were quietly speculating on just how long the city boy schoolteacher would last in the wilderness, Pepper was making every effort to help us adapt to our new way of life. On more than one occasion he provided the means that enabled us to make it from one day to the next during times of serious financial woes.

The move here, for instance, had taken all of our savings and thus throughout the first year the monthly stretches between paydays became the most difficult I had ever experienced in my life. "Desperate" is perhaps the most appropriate word.

Once, when the cupboard was totally bare save for baby food for Anna, I drove up to Villa de la Mina and asked Pepper for the loan of one of his rifles, making a concerted effort to convince him that my sporting blood had taken a rise and I wanted to do a little target practice and perhaps see if I could bring down a deer. The truth of the matter was that I was so panicked by our grocery situation at the time that I might well have attacked Bambi with bare hands in hopes of soon having meat on the table.

Not one to ask a lot of questions, Pepper nonetheless seemed to understand the situation I was in. "Ever done much hunting before?" he asked.

"Some," I said, hoping he would not recognize it as the bald-faced lie that it was.

As if I had not even answered his question, he proceeded to give me a quick beginner's course on the use of a rifle and suggested a particular spot on his ranch where I might be most likely to encounter a herd of mule deer.

"If you get one," he added, "bring him by here and I'll get some of the boys to help you dress him out. That's a pretty hard job for one person."

I suspicioned it would not have been for him, a man who no doubt had field-dressed many fallen game animals during his prospecting days. On the other hand, I seriously questioned whether I would have the ability — or the stomach — for the job myself. I told him I would appreciate his help.

With absolutely no nod toward modesty, I'm pleased to say that my initial attempt at hunting was successful; and in the month that followed, Olga fried, baked, broiled, stewed, and barbecued venison until we were all sick to death of it. The alternative, however, would no doubt have been even less palatable.

Then, two summers ago, before our second daughter, Cassandra, was born, we were facing a sizable medical and hospital bill without benefit of any insurance coverage. (When you're the principal, teacher, and janitor — a one man staff — it's no easy task to talk the school board into seeking out a group medical plan.)

Again Pepper came to the rescue, asking if I would be interested in working for him during the summer months as one of his guides. I had accompanied him on a few river floats and had helped out on occasion. With a little training, he suggested, I would be able to handle the rafts alone. The pay would be $15 a day, which sounded like a fortune since our only income other than my small salary at the time came from the loaves of molasses-and-honey bread that Olga baked and sold occasionally down at Ron and Shirley Willard's gas and grocery.

In addition to providing the funding for our second child, that first summer on the river was one of the most enjoyable and exciting experiences I've ever had. It was also the hardest $15 a day I've ever earned.

No amount of warning ever seems sufficient to convince first-time tourists of the demands of a two-day trip through the canyons where temperatures in the summer reach 120 degrees and the sand on the banks sends the thermometer reading beyond the 150-degree mark when the surface heat is measured. Regardless of the temperature, we would regularly advise the tourists to dress in long-sleeve shirts and long pants, but there were always those who assured us that long days on the tennis court or lounging by the pool back home had properly prepared them for long stretches of exposure to the sun. Without exception they would return to Villa de la Mina severely sunburned.

Pepper insists he has long since quit keeping count of the number of cameras and other personal items that have been lost overboard while the rafts were being negotiated through hazardous currents in the canyons. Rafts have capsized, been swamped, and have had the bottoms ripped out of them by sunken rocks from slides that occurred since the guide's last trip down the course. While Pepper's rides have, over the years, been tragedy free, there are countless stories of inexperienced adventurers drowning in attempts to negotiate the river and of people being lost for as long as a week before rangers from Big Bend National Park found them. Which is to say the river floats like those Villa de la Mina offers are not to be confused with a family outing to Disneyland. They are for the rugged and the athletic who come aboard fully aware of the very real possibility of danger.

"You ride the river on its terms," I've heard Pepper say many times. "Challenge it, and it'll swallow you up and spit you out in little pieces. We've got guides who aren't interested in risking anybody's life, their own or their passengers'. If it were otherwise, I'd have been out of business years ago, back to roaming these hills in search for that mercury deposit that's bound to be around somewhere."

In the two summers I worked regularly for Pepper (I still take an occasional group down one of the canyons when he's short-handed), I came to understand what he was talking about. I have yet to complete a trip down the river without an almost euphoric feeling of accomplishment. Bobbing and tossing through the white waters of the rapids and then, with the danger momentarily passed, suddenly coming into a still, calm stretch of water with rock canyon walls reaching hundreds of feet above you on both sides is an exercise in emotional Ping-Pong. At once one is made clearly aware of both the beauty and the tremendous power of nature.

Marcus, the youngest of the three Pepper children, was the first to finish his dinner and asked to be excused so that he might go outside and check on the goats before darkness set in. Very much his father's son, the cotton-headed six- year-old would, I'm certain, gladly choose the goat pen over my classroom any day.

Last spring he had started coming to school twice a week, on Mondays and Tuesdays, and I had given him a little kindergarten-level instruction. But he had not exactly fallen in love with the educational processes — more than once, in fact, he had pointed out to me that he would much rather be at home with his father, working with the goats. Still, Donna and I had agreed that since he would be coming to school regularly this year as a first-grader, it would do no harm for him to spend some time getting acquainted with a classroom situation.

In the mornings I would work with him on his ABCs and let him join the first-graders in their counting games, music, and art. But by noon each day he was longingly counting the minutes until time for school to be out. Which is not to say his first bit of part-time exposure to school was a total loss. Marcus Pepper perfected, far better than any student I've ever had, the art of soundly sleeping at his desk in the afternoons while the rest of the students busied themselves with the completion of their daily work.

His enthusiasm showed no great advancement this year as a first-grader. The first few weeks were very trying for him. He would cry. He would make dramatic efforts to convince Donna that he was desperately ill in the mornings and therefore should remain at home. The fact of the matter was he hated it.

He reminded me a great deal, in fact, of a first-grader I once knew named Trent Jones.

One afternoon as I tried to assure Donna that Marcus's reaction was nothing more than that of a normal six-year old boy, she replied by pointing out that Melissa, her seven-year-old daughter, had never once balked at attending school; had, as a matter of fact, started begging to go when she was four and a half. I advanced a rather clumsy theory that it was not unusual for little girls to show far more maturity than boys at that stage.

Pepper, who had been listening to the conversation without comment, realized that his wife was still uncomfortable, not completely buying my explanation, and made an effort to help. "It's just like little hound dogs," he explained. "The males are as dumb as rocks when they're puppies and the females seem to be born smart. Kids aren't much different." The look he received convinced me that neither Pepper nor I had managed to provide an anxious mother with any great degree of comfort with our cracker-barrel attempts to explain the maturation process of either children or hound dogs.

Still, once Marcus finally realized that he was in school this year to stay — tears, stubbornness, and all — he reluctantly accepted the fact that his carefree days of tending the goats and riding the Villa de la Mina burros were over and began to work alongside the other first-graders. He is now reading, turns in his papers on time, and cries only when I have to correct him for the occasional mischief he so delights in.

Melissa, now in the third grade and enjoying school to a degree her younger brother likely never will, joined her mother and Olga in clearing away the dishes while Pepper and I went into the den to build a fire in the big native rock fireplace that stretches the length of one wall. With the approach of night the dampness of the afternoon rain had returned to the air, seeming to rush the fall weather that would soon be upon us.

It didn't take long for our conversation to turn to the progress being made toward accreditation. Already Pepper had passed on my suggestion to try and convert the damaged cabin into a library and it had been met with approval by the other members of the school board. It looked, Pepper said, like the Terremar Corporation was even going to haul the building to the school grounds for us.

I updated him on my progress on the writing of the school board policies and told him of my occasional strong desire to make use of the rubber stamp Pam Gaddis had given me on some of the forms that suddenly seemed to be coming at me from all directions.

"I think," Pepper said, resting his boots on the brick ledge in front of the fireplace, "we're about to finally start making some headway on this thing."

"It's about time, don't you think?"

For a moment he did not answer, as if gathering his thoughts to be certain what he had to say was said right. "Trent, we've got pretty thankless jobs, you and me both. Folks expect a school-teacher to see to it their kids grow up with an education, and they

— a lot of them, anyway — don't much care how he goes about it so long as he keeps the children relatively happy and making decent grades. Being on the school board's not much different, really. Lotta folks around here don't even know what a member of the school board is supposed to do. They really don't care to be honest about it so long as their kids have a school to go to. I don't imagine it's really all that different in the big city.

"I know firsthand how discouraging it gets when you look around at everything that has to be done and see so many people standing around with their hands in their pockets, waiting for you to do it all. But that's the way it is, and the way it's likely to be until we whip this thing. I'll try to see that you get as much help from the school board as possible — we're all on the same side now — but on a lot of these matters we've got to lean on you just as hard as the next fella. We've got to depend on you to give us some direction because it gets a little complicated for us, too."

For Pepper, it was an exceptionally long speech. "How about the tax situation?" I asked.

"The county board in Alpine is looking into it and is supposed to let us know something shortly. What we're talking about is raising the tax rate from eighty cents per hundred acres to a dollar and a half a hundred. And instead of collecting tax on twenty-five percent of the value, they're considering jumping it to fifty percent. There'll be some ranchers scream to high heaven around here for a while, but they'll get over it. I've got to feel it will all come to pass. I can't see how they can afford not to agree to do it. It's something that's been needing doing for a long time.

Long before we got our tails in the crack we're in now."

I was greatly relieved to learn that attention was finally being focused on the tax situation.

"Olga and I have been doing whatever we can at the school to set things in order. I've added some more shelving and tried to organize the seating arrangement so that it will allow us the most room, but crowded is crowded any way you arrange it. I'm thinking that the cabin can be used for some classes when we get it fixed up. Some things, though, we simply can't handle until there are some funds to work with. For instance, we've got to have a new set of encyclopedias. You know what I've got down there right now?"

Pepper shook his head.

"I've got a set of Funk and Wagnalls, copyright nineteen forty-seven, with volumes number one and number twenty-five missing. I hardly think the accreditation people are going to be impressed to learn that we're still listing Harry S Truman as the president of the United States."

Pepper smiled. "Check and see what a new set will cost us. Maybe we can figure out some way to have it by the time we get your new library building ready to move into."

One of the first things I'd noticed when I initially came to Terlingua to interview for the teaching job was the desperate need for some semblance of a school library. As soon as I received word in San Antonio that the job was mine, I made an appeal to a couple of libraries for any books they might be planning to discard and then took out a small ad in the paper stating that a small one-room school in west Texas would appreciate any individual donations of used books for its library and offered to pick them up if people would just call me with an address. For a solid week after the ad ran I felt like a taxi driver, seeking out addresses where people would meet me at the door with cardboard boxes of books—children's books, books on science and history, dictionaries, paperbacks, and enough Gothic romances to keep Olga and every other woman in Terlingua in tears for some time to come. Before we ever made the move I traveled to Terlingua with a pickup loaded with books and materials for shelving. Thus was born our school library.

"I got a letter the other day," I told Pepper, "from the Texas Education Agency, saying it would be sending another representative out to visit us soon to evaluate the progress we've made."

"I hope he's an understanding man," Pepper said. "So do I."

At that particular moment neither Olga nor Donna could have cared whether the Texas Education Agency sent Attila the Hun to pass judgment on our school. Sitting in the kitchen, they were enthusiastically hatching elaborate plans for harvesting wild grapes in the spring for jelly making. Ten-year-old David sat with them at the table, listening in quiet fascination.

"Olga," I said, "we'd better gather up the kids and get on the road. Tomorrow's a school day."

David looked up and smiled. "I've already got my homework, Mr. Jones."

"Good for you. Are you practicing your reading in the book you brought home?"

He nodded.

Without exception, the most rewarding experiences I've had as a teacher have been with David. Slightly retarded, he had attended a special school in El Paso a couple of years after his mother and Pepper were married. He was seven when we moved to Terlingua, and I can still well remember the day Donna stopped by the house to introduce herself and talk with me about her son.

The opening of school was still a couple of weeks away and she asked if I would consider allowing David to enroll. In an honest, matter-of-fact manner she explained his problems and pointed out that the special-school instructors had unanimously discouraged her from attempting to send David to a public school. She openly admitted that she was unsure whether he could succeed in a normal classroom environment but was not yet ready to accept the advice of his former teachers without first allowing David a chance.

I explained to her that I had dealt with a number of slow learners in San Antonio and would naturally be happy to have David in school.

"Before you make a final decision to accept him," she said, "I'd like to have you meet David first. Maybe I could bring him by tomorrow afternoon."

"I'll look forward to seeing him," I told her.

He was a painfully shy child and could speak but a few words, none of them plainly. Most of his communication was done with either hand gestures or grunts. Still, I told his mother that

I expected to see him accompany the other children to school on enrollment day.

"It may go slowly for a while," I explained to her, "but I promise you that I'll make a special effort to do everything I can."

It was imperative, I felt, to first persuade David that he was no different than the other children, to treat him as much like the other first-graders as possible. Instilling some confidence in him, then, would be the initial step in his education.

That first year I had only ten students, so giving individual attention to each child was no problem. For long periods of time David and I would sit at his desk, reading books and looking at pictures and just talking. I wanted him to be exposed to as many words and sounds as possible. The next step would be to encourage him to begin using some of the words he was hearing over and over. I was pleased to find that he knew what most of the pictures were that we looked at and knew their names, but simply didn't have the vocabulary to say what they were. I could, for instance, ask him to point to a picture of a boat and he was immediately able to do it. I would then ask him to say the word "boat" and he would try, but with little early success. His eagerness and youthful determination, however, convinced me that with the proper degree of patience and persistence he would soon begin to show some progress.

In a couple of months he was talking some and identifying things around the classroom. In the meantime we began working on numbers, and I was again pleased to see him counting from one to ten in a relatively short time. I've heard gifted speakers deliver moving and eloquent lectures, have been exposed to a few persuasive men in pulpits, and listened as lyrical-voiced professors recited Carl Sandburg, but none ever impressed me as much as David did that first time he stood and clearly, slowly counted aloud from one to ten.

Once his vocabulary had expanded to about 100 words and he was able to write and recite the alphabet, I decided to start him on his first reader. Despite his advancement I wasn't altogether sure he was ready to take the step, but decided to let him have a try at it. At first the going was tedious at best. It took almost a month for him to master the first six-page story in the reader. For countless hours we would work on each word, sounding it out, writing it on paper, then on the blackboard. He would listen to me as I slowly read the short sentences, then I would listen as he attempted to do the same. I had a small cassette tape recorder from my college days and I taped the story and instructed David to take it home and sit and listen to it over and over.

Then one morning he arrived at school, bursting with excitement, informing me that he was ready to read his story to the class. He went through the entire six pages without a mistake, then broke into a wide, pleased grin. No doubt he had memorized it to some degree, but there was little question that he understood what he had read. When I took words from the story out of context he was quickly able to define them for me.

It was at that moment that I became convinced that David Thrift would prove to be an academic success.

He still doesn't progress as easily or as rapidly as the other students his age, but steady advancement is evident and I now believe he will one day graduate from a public high school and perhaps even go on to do well at some kind of trade school. David is the best example I can cite of a child who was able to start learning only after he first began to believe in himself and his abilities. The thing he most needed in the early stages of his academic development was something I was able, because of the small number of students, to give him — time. He needed a teacher who would not give up on him before he broke through some of the early barriers facing him. He needed someone who could take him through the early steps, over and over; someone who had the time for the painstaking repetition that was absolutely necessary. It is not a luxury teachers in the crowded big-city schools could have afforded him.

David is now reading at a second-grade level and can count to 200. He can add and subtract and is learning to write in cursive. He can learn to spell words in groups of as many as ten and talks constantly in a mixture of broken and complete sentences. And, even more important, I see his confidence growing daily.

As we drove the ten miles back home we saw that a near-full moon had replaced the late-afternoon rainbow, offering its own kind of spectacular show. Anna and Cassandra had fallen asleep only minutes after climbing into the pickup, and Olga and I were content to make the ride home in peaceful silence. The visit with the Peppers had been enjoyable and relaxing, and even though we had talked a great deal about the accreditation problems, I felt a welcome absence of pressure as I drove down the highway.

As we neared Study Butte the only lights remaining on in the short row of businesses were those coming from inside the cafe. "Willa's working late tonight," Olga observed. For a moment I considered stopping for a cup of coffee, then thought it might break the mood we were both in and didn't suggest it. Even seeing that Willa Ranallo was still working had brought a worried look from Olga.

Willa's fifteen-year-old daughter Irene had been one of my students, a pretty girl who made good grades, helped out with the younger children, and had on occasion served as a baby-sitter for us. But late in the summer she had learned that she was pregnant and she was now living in Alpine with friends until the baby came. She had had a long talk with Olga before leaving, assuring her that she wanted to have the child and promising to visit us on her occasional trips back home for weekends.

Though distressed that Irene was unwed and pregnant and moving away, Olga and I both agreed it was the best thing for her to get away, since the bitchiness of small town gossip was certain to spread. Even now, with Irene having been gone for almost two months, it was not hard to over-hear cruel speculations in the post office or at service stations about who the father of the baby might be.

I didn't need to ask to know that Olga was wondering about Irene. But obviously there was nothing we could do except give Willa and Irene our wholehearted support. We continued the ride home without saying a word, each deep in our own thoughts.

IX

There was much discussion on hiring another teacher. Glenn Pepper called the board into closed session to discuss the hiring of Olga Jones. After about 15 minutes they returned and announced they had decided to hire Olga Jones as a teacher's aide for Trent Jones... .

— From the minutes of a
Terlingua Common School Board meeting

As the pressures of the accreditation grew, I found my mood subject to sudden, often unpredictable change. One minute I would be at peace and happy, perhaps delighted by some academic problem solved at last by a struggling student. The next minute, as my thoughts turned to the list of demands from Austin and the creeping slowness with which they seemed to be being dealt with, I would come crashing down into a pitch-black funk.

There was still no word on any change in our tax structure, and my calls to Mayberry in Austin had been neither enlightening nor encouraging, though I did at least find out that he would be the one to inspect the school again. To add to the growing absurdity of the situation it had been necessary for the school board to borrow $4000 from the bank in Alpine to pay off the debt to the pump company that had installed the new water line in the fall and to be certain that my salary would be paid for the remainder of the year. Judge Thomas, God bless his forgetful soul, had failed to meet yet another deadline, thus causing the Texas Education Agency to withhold some much needed state funds until the papers were signed and received.

I was not, then, in the greatest of spirits as I returned from a visit to Ben Simmons. On the other hand, Olga was. I found her sitting at the kitchen table, laughing her head off.

"Heat finally getting to you?" I asked.

Still laughing, she could only shake her head and motion for me to sit with her. Finally she calmed down a bit. "Pam was just here," she said.

It was sufficient explanation. "What's new on the lunatic fringe?"

"She's painted another sign," Olga said. "This one's on the road to the post office, over where that old stop sign no one ever paid any attention to used to be. It says, 'Watch for Falling Cows.' Several cars have already stopped at Daisy's to ask what in the hell it means."

If you haven't already realized it, Pam Gaddis is, without serious challenge, Terlingua's resident hippie and screwball. The twenty-five-year-old daughter of an Alpine doctor, she lives just down the road from Daisy Adams in a small adobe house whose inside walls are covered with National Geographic pictures, but goes off to Colorado to work in the summers. If her constant good nature and devotion to fun and practical joking is a legitimate measure, I know of no one in the world who enjoys life more than Pam.

A few weeks ago, on her birthday, she'd arrived at the school on her multicolored bicycle with balloons for all the kids and a very official-looking petition seeking their wholehearted endorsement for her I Support Foolishness campaign. Needless to say, all signed.

Her greatest moments of glory, however, came after she had supplied the area with another of her highly professional but totally nonsensical signs. Following the chili cook-off, a broken down car had been abandoned by the side of the road near the ghost town and in the months that followed had become the target of vandals who shot out the windows, smashed fenders, and helped themselves to various working parts. By the time Pam set out to do her handiwork, the car was little more than a bullet hole-riddled shell. She very painstakingly printed a sign on the side of the car facing the highway, which read, "Rio Grande Bodyguard Service — The Quality of Our Work Speaks for Itself."

That does not, however, rank as my favorite piece of Pam's sign-painting mischief. That distinction is held by the job she did on yet another car which had been badly wrecked near the Lajitas Trading Post. On its only unmangled door she had painted, "Big Bend Auto Tours — Safe, Reliable Drivers."

"Maybe," I suggested to Olga, "I could get her to go out to that cabin the Terremar Corporation gave us and paint a big sign on the side of it, saying, 'Please Move Me to the Schoolgrounds – Immediately.' Otherwise, it looks as if it's going to rot before we ever get it."

My patience had just about expired on the matter. First it was thought that the Terremar people were going to move it. They hadn't. The school board was going to move it. They hadn't. Everyone in Brewster County, it seemed, was going to move it. But nobody did.

"Daisy mentioned something the other day about some

man who owns a big flatbed truck who told her he had seen the building and would move it up here for three hundred and fifty dollars," Olga said.

"Hell, that sounds reasonable to me."

"You got three hundred and fifty you can spare?" she replied.

Taking a sip from her iced-tea glass, I smiled, feeling no need to answer the question she well knew the answer to. "We've got to get that building up here. All I need is for

Mayberry to drop by one of these days soon and see us still packed into that classroom like so many bilingual sardines and figure I was just blowing smoke about all our big expansion plans. And Mayberry or not, we've got to have some more room. Daisy ought to realize that about as well as anyone."

Her two nieces, Sharon and Tommi Ann Hill, had moved to Terlingua after Christmas to live with their grandmother, Evelyn Fulcher, while their mother completed her nurse's training back home in Houston. Their arrival had caused a trip to Pepper's to retrieve the last remaining desks that were in storage.

"Any suggestions?" Olga asked.

"I think," I told her, "it's about time for the Bingo Bandits to ride again."

In the past when the need had arisen for projects that our budget could not accommodate — like the weather station we had erected on the school grounds one year, or a new flag to replace one shredded by the same windstorm that had lifted the roof off the post office and replaced it in Daisy's picture window – I had called on our loosely organized Parents' Club for fund raising help. The favorite sources of income had always been bake sales and Bingo nights at the school.

"We'll shoot the works on this one," I said. "We'll have Bingo and a bake sale at the same time. You're in charge of seeing to it that all the mothers bake something. I'll handle the Bingo."

After checking out the Parents' Club's bank balance, Donna Pepper assured me that a good turnout at the Bingo and a brisk sale of pies and cakes should bring the total to a sufficient level to pay for the moving of the cabin.

"Why," I asked Olga, "didn't I think of this two months ago?"

"Probably," she said, "because you haven't had time."

Sitting adjacent to the school, on its foundation of old railroad ties, it was a magnificent sight. It would not only provide room for an adequate library but, equally important, would provide added class space. Olga would be able to take the younger children there for reading and music, and it could also house the portable science laboratory that would be ordered as soon as Judge Thomas got around to signing his name so that the state funds would be released. Remodeling of the Terlingua School Annex and Library began immediately. A small bathroom was the most seriously damaged part of the building and would, I decided, need to be completely torn out. So one afternoon, as Olga taught the rest of the students, I collected several of the older boys — Carlos Armendariz, Jerry Williams, Matt Simmons, and Keith Ferris — and solicited their help in tearing the walls and fixtures of the room away. While it is generally necessary to constantly supervise and instruct when attempting to teach youngsters how to build something, it is amazing how much instinctive knowledge they have about tearing things up. They attacked their chore with great enthusiasm and had the job completed in time to go over to the house and clean up before time for school to be dismissed.

With the reality of the library, a renewed enthusiasm toward the school quickly spread from the children to their parents. Almost daily, mothers would drop by or send notes saying they would be glad to help out. Ernie Harmon volunteered to help me repair the paneling that had been pulled away from the walls in the earlier accident the cabin had experienced. That done, we built shelves. Donna Pepper, Mrs. Acosta, and Olga painted and cleaned and the students pitched in to move the books into the new library. I set to work building a big desk which would sit in the middle of the room. It was, all in all, a fine addition, something everyone who had helped to make a reality could be proud of.

I found myself wishing Cactus Jack Hollis had been there to lend a hand and maybe donate a few of his desert rocks to be placed along some of the freshly painted shelves. A colorful old character who lived for years in one of the adobe remains in the ghost town, he used to occasionally ride one of his burros down to the school to visit and always seemed delighted when he would find me engaged in some kind of work he could lend a hand at.

He was, in fact, one of the first people I met after arriving in Terlingua. I was cleaning the school prior to registration, struggling to get a large old rug, weighted by years of dirt and dust, out of the building, when he rode up. After silently watching for a minute, he slid down off his mount, introduced himself, and offered a solution to my problem. He instructed me to tie one end of his rope to the rug while he secured the other around the waist of his burro and then let the weary-looking but obliging animal do my work for me. Hollis was a rambling conversationalist who often boasted to passing tourists that he could, through sheer grit and knowledge of the land, live quite comfortably for long stretches with nothing but a bag of dry beans to supplement the food he foraged from the desert. He managed to earn a scrimpy living by selling cactus and rock, which he would travel far out into the desert to gather and pack back to his ghost-town home on his burro.

A slight man with skin leathered brown by years under the broiling summer sun, he always looked to me like something out of one of the Grade B westerns I remember watching as a boy. I can't recall ever seeing him when he wasn't wearing a pair of leather chaps, a dusty black hat with a snakeskin band, and both gun and knife hanging from his belt.

His father, who lived in a rest home in Alpine, died last year and shortly thereafter Cactus Jack quietly left, saying goodbye to no one.

His departure leaves only Severiana Hinojos still living in Terlingua proper. She too lives alone in one of the tiny adobe buildings and just recently celebrated her ninety-ninth birthday. Her father, husband, and several brothers worked for Howard

Perry when the Chisos Mining Company was still in operation. I have often regretted the fact that she speaks absolutely no English, so I would not understand her marvelous stories about this country and its history.

One evening last fall, when Olga was holding one of her occasional night adult-education classes at the school, Mrs. Hinojos arrived, having been brought by one of her daughters, and explained that she wished to learn to write her name. Olga, aware of the woman's failing eyesight, gave her a large felt marker and slowly, patiently showed her how to form the proper letters. Mrs. Hinojos sat in the back of the room practicing through the two-hour class, and left smiling, taking with her the papers she had been writing on and the marker Olga had given her. Her need for formal education evidently satisfied, she never attended another class.

It is only fair that I point out that one feature of the new library failed to exactly thrill Olga. The small windows in the converted cabin were not adequate to allow what I considered the proper amount of ventilation in the room, so I borrowed the air cooler from Olga's kitchen and' placed it in the library. When she discovered what I had done, she lectured me at length on my long-standing habit of robbing Peter to pay Paul and suggested in less than loving terms that I might like to cook dinner in her "steam bath" kitchen.

All seemed forgiven a few days later, however, when, at the first school board meeting held in the new library, the board formally voted to hire her to officially serve as the teacher's aide required by the Texas Education Agency. I was a bit surprised at her excitement over being hired to a job she had already been working at most of the year anyway. But the difference, she explained, was that now she was going to be paid.

That, I agreed, did make a difference. Word had finally come that the state funds would soon be forthcoming. It would be enough to see us through the rest of the year, including paying Olga's salary.

After the board meeting adjourned, Pepper and I sat in the library talking while Olga got the kids ready for bed. On the table sat the list of items Mayberry had told us must be completed if we hoped to gain accreditation.

"Seems to me," he said, "we're finally getting to a point where we can check a few of these things off. Maybe it's time for me to give Mayberry a call and let him know where we stand."

The physical feat of moving the cabin and putting it in workable order stood as one of the first visible signs of accomplishment to many and represented to Pepper and the other board members a giant step forward. "The added space and the hiring of Olga and all those nit-picking things like writing up an agenda for school board meetings are taken care of," he continued. "Where do you think we stand now?"

"A helluva lot better than we were six months ago, but I'm not sure what it all adds up to aside from the fact that some of the things we've done have considerably upgraded the school. That in itself is an accomplishment not to be taken lightly, but I don't know to what extent it's going to impress the people in Austin."

I leaned over and pointed to one of the items on the list.

"Money's still the big thing. 'A realistic financial plan which will be in operation this incoming tax year,' it says. Bingo and bake sales aren't what they're talking about. Unless the new tax alignment gets the okay before summer and we can show them a budget that will insure our being able to handle our financial affairs far better than we've been able to up to now, everything else we've done won't amount to a hill of beans. Lord only knows what they'd think if they knew we had to borrow money from the bank just to get us through until the state money got here."

Pepper smiled. "I found out the other day," he said, "that we did the impossible on that transaction. Maybe even violated another rule or two."

"How's that?"

"I was reading through one of the books on Texas school law the other night and came across a rule that clearly states that no school or school district can borrow money from a bank without having first put it to a vote of all registered voters in the school district," he said.

"And the guy at the bank didn't say anything about it?" "I guess he hadn't read the book either."

"Good God, if we keep working at it, we won't have to worry about what happens to the school. They're going to come with handcuffs and cart us all off to jail."

We both laughed at what was far from a laughing matter. With the additional expense of paying Olga a monthly salary, the cost of the new science laboratory, and the regular operating expenses to be expected, the Terlingua School District could, to the best of my figuring, end the year with a grand total of $214 in the bank.

"That won't even buy the encyclopedias we need," I said. "Unless the tax money increases, we aren't going to be able to open the doors of this place even if they let us. We'll be too broke to pay attention, much less my salary. The school board is going to have to get with the county commissioner and get the ball rolling. Everyone tells me he's sympathetic to our problems and that he's on our side in this thing. He just needs a little shove to get things under way."

Pepper, as usual, saved the worst news for last. "It's going to be a while," he said. "Judge Hernandez, the county commissioner, died just the other day. They'll have to elect a new one — Lord only knows who — before they're likely to get too high behind doing anything else."

Saying nothing, I rose and walked outside where the quiet was interrupted only by an occasional high-pitched bark from Samantha as she chased a rabbit across the moon-shadowed desert. Her chances of catching that prairie-wise animal, I thought, were probably about as good as ours seemed to be of ever getting a leg up on our problem.

Pepper, his hands stuffed into the hip pockets of his jeans, joined me.

"Seems like every time we take a step or two forward," I observed, squinting my eyes in hopes of seeing what progress Samantha might be making in her pursuit, "we take about the same number backward."

"Seems that way," he agreed, "but the way I look at it, it beats the hell out of standing still."

"Pepper," I said, "if you're not careful, people around here are going to be calling you the sage of Terlingua."

"I've been called a lot worse," he smiled. "It's getting late; I'd better be going."

I stood in the warm night air, watching as his headlights disappeared down the road, past the cattle guard and onto the highway. In the distance, Samantha had stopped barking. She had given up the chase. But not, I thought, before having made a hell of a race out of it.

The annual arrival of spring calls up new energies among schoolchildren. The basic, repetitious processes of learning shift gears as more emphasis is placed on creative endeavors by which they can begin to measure the facts that conjugation, spelling, and long division have been learned. There also seems each spring to be an increase in outside involvement in the activities of the school and the students. Mothers bring fresh-baked cookies to be handed out for the students to have with their sack lunches. Fathers, seldom seen in the fall and winter, bring the children to school and then congregate at the cafe for coffee and speculation on the heights oncoming summer temperatures will reach.

The school in Big Bend Park had called, inviting us to attend a presentation of Cinderella, prompting the need to borrow Daisy's station wagon since my pickup would no longer accommodate the entire student body as it once had. Snake Smith, proud member of the American Legion, came by to tell the students of an essay contest on "Americanism" that was to be held. "You young folks," he said, "just write in twenty-five words or less what you think Americanism is all about and we'll give out a prize for the best one. We'll be having a barbeque later in the spring and will announce the winner then."

Marcus Pepper was among the first to seize on the essay contest to speak his piece. "In America," he wrote, "you can raise all the goats you want to." Having made his statement, he felt no need to use the fourteen words remaining to him to mention anything about the nation's mandatory education requirement.

Her first paycheck in her hand, Olga was smiling broadly. "Let's splurge," she suggested.

"How about a trip around the world?"

"No, Dallas. Let's take a trip to Dallas over the spring break. I've never been there. We could visit some of the friends we've met on the river floats and at the chili cook-offs. It would be fun and I could do a little shopping. I'd like to get some new guitar strings and a new bra and some new shoes for the girls. I might even buy you something."

I considered suggesting a new air cooler for the kitchen but thought better of it. That dog had finally been set to sleep and was best left to lie. "Sounds good to me," I said.

Thus we would finally spend a few days away from Terlingua and school and accreditation problems. Needless to say, it was an enjoyable respite.

When we returned home, however, the answer to a letter I had written the Texas Education Agency was waiting at the post office.

Jack Mayberry, it seemed, felt no need to make a second inspection of our school.

X

Billy was up in front of the class, giving his book report, when the telephone in the back of the room rang. It was his mother, wanting to know if he had any idea where her big iron Dutch oven might be. She needed it right away. So I got Billy's attention, relayed the question to him, and he stopped in the middle of his report to remind his mother that she had loaned it to one of the neighbors. He then resumed his report without the slightest hitch.

I knew Trent wouldn't mind my interrupting one of his students since it sounded like an emergency.

— Olga Jones

For several weeks there had been a gradually increasing display of unrest among the students; an inability to concentrate on either the daily class work or the minimal homework they were assigned. As the school year drew to a close the already oppressive desert heat drained ambition and energies. Daydreams of a summer of freedom from academic pursuits made the simplest of classroom tasks a chore for many of the youngsters. Even I was finding it hard to keep my mind on the lesson plans that I'd so laboriously drawn up.

Fifth-grader Irma Madrid, whose English had shown marked improvement since the beginning of the school year, summed up the feelings of most of the students during lunch one day. Olga noticed her sitting at her desk, not touching her sandwich, and staring out the window. "Irma," Olga asked, "are you feeling all right?"

Irma sighed and nodded her head.

"But something seems to be the matter," Olga pursued. "Oh, Mrs. Jones," Irma finally admitted, "I feel like I've been going to school all my life."

It was not, however, the drudgery of the final days of the school year nor the anticipation of a carefree summer that occupied my mind; it was the fate of the school itself that was causing me grave concern. My optimism was spent, though I had not admitted it to Olga, and the thought of the children having to travel all the way to Alpine by bus each day the following fall, of my having to seek work elsewhere, of there being no school in Terlingua, had weighed on me heavily for several weeks.

I finally ran out of patience and placed a call to Jack Mayberry in Austin to ask when the Education Board would make its final decision on the accreditation. Mayberry hesitated at first, obviously attempting to avoid the issue, but when pressed he finally said, "Mr. Jones, as a personal friend I would advise you to look for another job. The fact of the matter is that I don't see any way this matter is going to be positively resolved. I'm sure you will be receiving a letter shortly which will outline the whole thing in detail, but it might be of some help to you to know now. A man of your abilities and reputation will have no trouble finding another position. I would suggest that you wait until the letter arrives before you tell the members of your school board of the decision."

I thanked Mayberry and slowly put the receiver back in its cradle. Standing silently for a moment in the privacy of the bedroom, I could hear the muffled sounds of the children at play on the school grounds where Olga was overseeing recess. "Goddammit," I said, "I don't want another position."

The remainder of the school day crept by. I went about my duties in a rote manner. When finally the day was over and all the students had left, Olga and I sat in the classroom sharing a large glass of iced tea she had brought from the house. "We've worked our butts off for nothing," I said, making no attempt to mask my disappointment. "I really thought we were going to make it, to show them that we could meet all the requirements, but they had their minds made up from the beginning. They never planned to give us a chance."

Olga sat quietly as my emotions hopscotched from disappointment to discouragement to anger. She said I looked more tired than she had ever seen me. "Did Mayberry say it was official — that the decision had been made?"

"He gave me that impression, but I'd have to guess that they haven't even considered our case yet. He'll probably tell Phillips now that we're getting anxious and they'll dig our file out from somewhere and write a letter telling us that after careful consideration they've decided to turn down our request for accreditation."

"It's not fair," Olga said. "Nothing much is," I replied.

"What are we going to do now?" Olga asked.

I did not answer immediately. It was not something I had thought about, my total concentration for months having been directed toward the survival of the school I had worked at for four years. Finally I rose from my desk, shoved my hands into my jeans, and forced a smile. "First," I said, "I'm going to go tell the members of the school board and see if they have any ideas I haven't thought of. Then we're going to finish out the school year just as if nothing had ever happened."

"You're not going to give up, are you?" Olga said. It was more a statement of fact than a question.

"It's too late to give up." I bent over and kissed her on the forehead. "I'll be back in a couple of hours."

As I walked into the afternoon sun toward the pickup, Olga stood in the doorway of the school watching me. "Trent," she yelled as I opened the pickup door. I turned to see what she wanted. "I love you," she said. I waved back and climbed into the truck to carry the bad news to the members of the school board.

Glenn Pepper was bathed in perspiration, engaged in his unending battle with a faulty jeep motor, when I arrived. "If I can get this damn thing running," he said, "I think I'm going to drive it over the hill and into one of the mine shafts. Then maybe hire me a couple of wetbacks to close off the entrance."

"I'd think twice about it," I said. "Bad as that one is, it's the best one you've got."

"I guess you're right," Pepper admitted. "I just wish I'd been born with a little more mechanical know-how."

Neither of us, however, was one for prolonged small talk, so I got down to business. I told Pepper of the phone conversation with Mayberry.

"What do we do next?" he asked.

"I was hoping you might have some ideas."

"It all comes down to money, doesn't it?" Pepper said. "We've done everything they asked, to the letter. We've gone right down that damn list, one-two-three. But the fact that we don't have money in the bank is making everything else a waste of time. What we need is a fairy godmother or something."

"Or something," I said. "It doesn't sound good, Glenn. Are you willing to keep fighting this thing?" "Sure, but how?"

"They told me we can appeal whatever decision the accreditation board makes. That might not do anything but drag this thing on for a few more months, but, hell, we've gone this far with it, we might as well fight it to the end. But I'm not going to do it alone. If the members of the board say they'll back me, I'll do whatever else I can. "

"I'll see to it that everyone backs you," Pepper said. "Let's go in and get a beer."

"I've got to be going," I said. "I'm going to try to get by and see the other members of the board."

As we talked, Donna Pepper appeared with two beers in her hand. "It looked like this conversation was pretty serious," she said, "so I thought you two might like something cool."

Her husband briefly outlined to her what I had been telling him. She listened with a sad face. "I've been afraid all along that it would happen."

"We're not whipped yet," I said, defiantly.

Donna looked at me, saying nothing. Finally she smiled, nodded, and said she had to attend to something in the kitchen. "If you two don't have sense enough to come in out of the sun, just yell if you need another beer. Trent, tell Olga and the kids hello, and, you guys, don't be such strangers." As she walked away Glenn's mouth drew taut. "If this comes about," he said, "we all lose, don't we? The kids lose their school, you lose your job – and I lose my family."

I knew what Pepper was saying. Every cent the Peppers had was invested in Villa de la Mina and they had spent bone wearying years turning it into a profit-making operation. To give it up now and move from Terlingua would mean throwing ten years of sweat and sacrifice out the window. Since the possibility of the school closing had first come up they had talked at length of the alternatives. They had agreed they would not subject their children to a 160 mile round-trip bus ride every day, and thus it had been decided that if, in fact, the school closed, Donna and the children would move to Alpine and live in an apartment during the school year, returning to Terlingua on the weekends.

"I'll bring the kids in to school in the morning," Pepper told me now, "and we'll call Phillips and tell him we're not ready to take no for an answer."

Ben Simmons had continuously been the most optimistic member of the board; indeed over the past several months he'd become the self-appointed cheerleader for the board members and me. "Those people," he had often said, "came out here originally and saw our situation and figured us to be like a lot of other little schools. They figured we'd just give up and take our licking. No way they can't be impressed by what's been done. They'll have to give us that accreditation."

I found Ben working at the Lajitas Trading Post. Because of the optimism he had maintained throughout the effort, he took the news hardest. "I can't believe it," he said. "I just can't believe they could do something like this. It's not fair. Dammit, Trent, you've done a lot of hard work, a helluva lot more than any of us had the right to expect from you."

I told Ben of my conversation with Pepper and explained the legal recourse of appealing the decision. Ben assured me that he was ready to continue the battle. Unlike Pepper and me, though, he did not see the problem as basically a matter of money.

"You know, Trent, what this whole mess boils down to is politics. Just like everything else. Back when I was living in Midland, that's the way it all worked. If you wanted something done right in Austin, you had to know somebody. Let's get busy and see if we can't find somebody that'll be willing to give our cause a few kind words in the right places there in the capitol building."

"You know anybody, Ben?" I asked.

"Not offhand."

"Neither do I," I said. "I'll be in touch."

It was almost dark and the task of being a bearer of bad news had wearied me. I decided I would wait until later to tell Daisy of the call. I already knew what her reaction would be; she had already admitted that she felt the whole campaign was a lost cause. "This is the same bull they used to give me at the post office all the time," she'd said at one of the school board meetings. "Those people have one-track minds. They were always wanting me to run my post office the same way Dallas runs theirs. They never had any conception of how life is out here, and no amount of talking and arguing is gonna persuade them to change their minds." Clearly Daisy had given up. And while I needed her help and support, I could not blame her.

I had heard her talk often of the numerous times they had almost lost the school for reasons ranging from decline in student enrollment to the almost impossible task of finding a teacher willing to work for the small wages they were able to pay. Somehow, each crisis had been overcome until now. But that was when Daisy Adams was younger and still possessed of a fighting spirit. At seventy-four she preferred to avoid, whenever possible, anything that might disrupt the quiet flow of the life she'd been living since her retirement from her job as postmaster.

Olga and I sat up late that evening discussing what exactly should be said the following morning when Pepper called Phillips from the telephone in the schoolhouse. "We have a right to a second visit," I told her, "so that we can show them firsthand the improvements we've made. And we have to take a firm position on Sam Thomas's irresponsibility. We need to tell them that we've done everything we can and are ready to do more if they will just come down here and tell us what it is we need to do."

Olga agreed and smiled. "This afternoon," she said, "I was afraid you were ready to say to hell with it and give up."

"I think I was," I replied. "But not now?" "Not now."

The following morning Pepper arrived with David and Melissa. We tried to call Phillips's office, but as was so often the case the phone was out of order. It would probably be several days before whatever repairs were necessary would be made. We decided to wait.

In a few days a letter arrived from Phillips's office. In it he outlined all of the shortcomings that had been noted during Mayberry's original visit, making no reference to knowledge that corrective efforts had been made. The terse, formally written letter ended with the following paragraph: "In view of the number and seriousness of the violations of accreditation standards described in the report, the following recommendation is made: It is recommended that the Terlingua Common School District be denied accreditation."

By the time of its arrival the school board members and I had agreed it would serve no good purpose to make the decision public. "There's no need for everybody, parents and kids alike, to get themselves depressed over all this until we're sure we've had our last bat," Simmons had said. "We'll get busy seeing what can be done, and in the meantime, Trent, you carry on at school as if nothing has happened."

Secrets, however, are not long kept in a small town and within days there was the uneasy rumor that Terlingua would be without a school the following fall. But since no official word had come from me or the board, the students and many of their parents seemed satisfied that such a decision was not definite. Olga and I both were careful not to even mention the problem to the students, and they, in turn, as if taking the cue from their elders, seldom brought it up. On those occasions when someone would inquire about the status of the school, I would simply say it had not yet been decided.

It was not a problem the children paid much attention to anyway, since their thoughts were now occupied with preparations for the annual Spring Happening. An end-of-the-year pageant directed by Olga, it was the social highlight of the season. This year Olga had decided to convert several Rudyard Kipling stories into plays and have the students act them out. There would also be singing and dancing.

While Olga worked with the younger children, I got the older students busy with the construction of a stage. For the last couple of weeks of school I altered the classroom routine, spending the mornings on regular studies and leaving afternoons free for rehearsal and other preparations.

The enthusiasm of the students returned immediately after my announcement of plans for the event, and their eagerness rubbed off on me. Olga and I became so involved in the preparations that little time was left to contemplate the ominous problem that hung over the school.

"This," Olga told me, "is going to be the best Spring Happening we've ever had. Maybe we should send an invitation to Mr. Phillips and see if he can come down here and see what our kids can do."

I laughed. "I think it would be best to keep his name off the invitation list. We don't want him showing up and spoiling the thing."

He would no doubt have been hard pressed to find a seat anyway. From all indications, everyone in Terlingua was planning to come — even several local residents who held no fondness for me or the manner in which I ran the school. The day before the dress rehearsal I sent notes home with all of the students who lived outside walking distance of the school, urging their parents to allow them to stay the night with Olga and me since last-minute rehearsals and preparations would likely continue into the night. The boys would sleep on pallets in the house with me, the note explained, and the girls would sleep in the schoolhouse with Olga.

The parents unanimously agreed to the adventuresome proposal.

Aside from the fact that rehearsal was interrupted once when Anna, playing outside, sat on an anthill and suffered several painful but not serious stings, and aside from the fact that Olga broke a string on her guitar — the last of the ones she had purchased on our trip to Dallas — and aside from a bit of off-key harmony that it was too late to do anything about, the evening went well.

As the children were finally preparing for bed, Billy Ranallo sought out Olga, explaining that he had something he wanted to tell her. His eyes danced as he took her hand and led her out of earshot of the rest of the children. For several days, Olga had watched him carefully, aware that he was worried about his sister. The last word Olga had received was that Irene's baby was long overdue.

"Mrs. Jones," Billy said in a rush that caused his words to run together, "Irene had her baby. Mama told me to tell you first thing this morning, but I wanted to wait until you weren't busy."

Olga grabbed him and surrounded him with a hug, then hurried him over to the house where I was getting everyone settled. "Trent, come out here, quick," she said. "Billy has some wonderful news."

"She had a little boy," Billy said proudly, "and named him Matthew Mark."

"Is Irene feeling okay?" I asked.

"Mama says she's feeling just fine and she'll be coming home pretty soon. Brother Bob is coming to christen the baby."

"Billy, that's the most wonderful news I've had in a long time," Olga said. "Thank you for saving it for a time in the day when we weren't so busy."

"That's okay. I've just about been busting all day to tell somebody, but I wanted to tell you first. Goodnight."

"I'll be in in a minute," I said. "Get ready for bed. We've got a busy day tomorrow."

As Billy went inside to join the others on their makeshift beds scattered about the house, Olga and I stood in the fast cooling night air for a few moments.

"Isn't it wonderful?" Olga said finally. "Irene will need a lot of help at first, but she'll make a really good mother."

"I think she'll do fine," I agreed.

"I should think so," Olga said in mock sternness. "After all, her new baby has two pretty good godparents to look after it." Irene had asked us to be the child's godparents several months earlier and we had told her we'd be delighted. We stood in silence for a while, gazing out at the mountains and the multitude of stars that formed a halo over their peaks. I finally broke the silence. "Damn," I said, "I feel like celebrating."

"What you had better do," Olga said, "is get in the house and play baby-sitter before your guests wreck the place."

By 7:30 the following evening a permanent cloud of dust hung over the road leading to the school as residents made their way to the Spring Happening. Ernie Harmon had volunteered to cook spaghetti for the event and was delightedly heaping large helpings onto the paper plates of the arriving guests while his wife served iced tea. Many of the adults grasped the opportunity to visit with fellow residents they had not seen for weeks while the children, all freshly dressed in their costumes of light blue T-shirts and jeans (for the boys) and light blue blouses and jean skirts (for the girls), hurried about making the last-minute preparations for the production. A member of the American Legion was on hand to present Christina Farris with a medal for her winning essay on Americanism.

If the Terlingua Common School District was, in fact, breathing its final breath, it was going to go out with a yell and not a whimper.

A standing-room-only crowd watched as the Spring Happening proceeded amid much singing, laughter, and applause. What the singing lacked in proper pitch and tone it made up for in vigor and spirit. Olga accompanied the songs on her guitar, and no one seemed to notice that it was minus one string. Neither did they seem bothered when the younger students became sudden victims of amnesia and had to be repeatedly prompted during the play.

When the affair finally came to an end with a brief speech by me about the dedication and hard work of the students, it was close to midnight. The loudest cheer of the evening came from the children themselves when I announced that, since the show had lasted so long, school would not begin the following day until ten o'clock.

The last day of school, then, would be a short one.

A procession of obviously proud parents filed past us, thanking us one by one for our efforts on behalf of their children. Several, aware of the letter from Phillips, asked if there was anything they could do. "We'll let you know," I found myself saying repeatedly.

One of the last to leave was Daisy Adams. As the procession of cars and pickups slowly made its way to the highway, a crawling stream of light in the pitch-dark of the moonless night, she waited outside, talking with several remaining visitors, then sought me out.

"I've seen a lot of things put on by the kids of this school," she said, "but tonight's was the best ever. You and Olga have a right to be proud. So do the kids. Everybody in this dried-up little ol' town ought to. I know I am. I just wanted you to know that."

She smiled and gave me a hug, then pulled a piece of folded paper from her purse. "It's something my niece wrote," she said. "It made me stop and do some serious thinking about things."

She stuffed it into my shirt pocket, told Olga to bring the kids and come for the day as soon as she could get free, then walked out to her car.

When the last of the visitors had left, Olga and I sat and drank in the quiet. "I think," Olga said, "everyone had a good time. The Spring Happening was a rip-roaring success."

I only nodded. I was reading the paper Daisy had given me. It was written in a neat but childish hand and addressed to Mr. Phillips and Mr. Mayberry, 201 East 11th Street, Austin, Texas.

> *Dear Sirs:*
> *I am a student from the Terlingua School House, my teacher being Mr. Jones.*
> *School is different here. I am learning a lot more here than in any other school.*
> *Mr. Jones works hard with us and he explains our lessons more clearly than any other teachers. When we learn something at this school we practically never forget it.*
> *Mr. Jones makes our lessons more interesting. That makes me interested in the subject. Other teachers bore me and I don't learn anything.*
> *I think this school is wonderful.*
> *I think you have to be a student here to be able to know how great this school is.*
> *Yours cordially, Tommi Ann Hill*

Olga read it and smiled. "I don't know whether we should give it back to Daisy and let her mail it, or have it framed and hung on the wall."

"We're going to let her mail it," I said. "Along with any other letters I can get people around here to write. It may not do any good, but I can't see at this point where it could hurt."

The final morning of the school year was spent cleaning up the debris left from the Happening and checking in books. By lunchtime all the necessary chores had been accomplished.

"Okay," I said, "everybody get their lunch bag and go out and get in the pickup. We're going to the creek for a picnic and a swim."

In a matter of minutes thirty children were piled onto the truck, spilling onto the hood and the top of the cab. Traveling along at a snail's pace, the amusing sight caught the attention of several passersby who stopped to watch as the celebrating collection of yelling, laughing bodies crept along the road leading to Terlingua Creek.

For the next couple of hours the students frolicked in the shallow water of the creek, sang songs accompanied by Olga's minus-one-string guitar, listened as Bubba told an endless string of elephant jokes he had not been able to tell during the previous night's program. Ruth Staton, having seen the procession headed toward the creek earlier, stopped by with candy for all the kids and laughed heartily as several of the older boys tried without success to throw their teacher into the water.

Finally I signaled everyone back onto the truck. "Back to the schoolhouse," I ordered. "We're going to have a test." Though no one believed me, there were loud moans nonetheless.

Back in the schoolroom, the children settled down at their desks and I handed out the report cards. To the surprise of no one, there were no failures. "Many of your parents won't be here until three-thirty to pick you up," I said, "but I'm going to dismiss you early so you can visit with each other for an hour or so. You can stay here in the building or go out onto the school grounds."

For a moment no one moved. It was as if they could not believe the school year was suddenly over. "School," I said with dramatic flourish, "is out for the summer."

Tommi Ann was the first to start crying. Then Suzy Farris. Iselda, who had never attended any other school in her eight years of education, could no longer hold back the tears. Jerry Williams, his face flushed, excused himself to go to the back room.

"That's enough of this," I said. "This is supposed to be a happy day. Everybody outside."

The students hesitated briefly, then began to slowly file through the door.

It would be left to Suzy Farris to ask the question that was on the minds of all the students. Waiting until everyone was out of the room, she approached me.

"Mr. Jones," she asked, "is there going to be a school here next year?" For the first time the question was put forth with the straightforwardness and simplicity that only a child possesses.

I looked down at her and placed my arm around her shoulder. "Suzy," I said, "I don't know."

XI

When Olga's mother came to Terlingua to pay her daughter a visit shortly after their move there, she was taken aback by the lifestyle her daughter had chosen to pursue. Looking at the milk goat that Trent had earlier purchased, Irene Rithianos shook her head and heaved a sigh of resignation. "Olga," she said, "we moved to this country from Greece when you were just four years old. We came to America to get away from living like this and here you are with no water, no money, and a milk goat."

"I know, Mama," Olga replied, "and I'm very happy."

Wearied by the events of the year and resigned to the fact that I had done all I could to hold the school's fragile future together, I put my records in order, gave the schoolhouse a thorough cleaning, and locked it. Then I suggested to Olga that this summer might be a good time to pay a visit to her parents in New Jersey.

Olga had been talking about going home for a visit for the past several years and it was one of those things we had hoped to do on several previous occasions, but there always seemed to be something to force another year's postponement. This summer I was determined that nothing would be allowed to ambush the plans.

Olga, obviously delighted both at the prospect of the cross country trip and the reunion with her parents, was nevertheless somewhat surprised at my seemingly snap decision to leave when everything was still up in the air. "We don't have to go this summer," she offered. "Mom and Dad will understand."

"It's a good time to do it," I replied. "I'm ready to get away from people asking me if there is going to be a school next year, like it's my decision to make. I'm going to leave it with them. Hell, I've done everything I can short of holding a gun to a few people's heads. If they want a school here next year, they've still got a couple of months to do something about it. The school board knows what has to be done between now and the meeting in August. We'll go see your parents for a while, then travel down to Corpus and see my folks, and then be in Austin in time for the hearing — if there is a hearing."

Thus after tending to all the trivial but necessary duties related to leaving home for an extended period — Olga asked Daisy if she would water her plants occasionally; I made the rounds to tell several people I was taking a summer vacation and, if the need arose, could be reached at my in-laws' home — I gathered my family and did one of the hardest things I had ever done in my life.

To some, even Olga, though she did not admit it, it appeared that the determined, often stubborn and unbending young teacher had finally come to the end of his rope and was now eloping from the tedious problem he had been wrestling with for so many months.

Such was not the case. Rather, the trip was a carefully calculated, well-thought-out grandstand play, a gamble, to be sure, but one I felt stood as my last resource. Several hundred miles of driving were behind us before I explained my motives to my concerned wife.

As Anna and Cassandra, having grown bored with the books and toys they had brought along, fell into the rhythmic breathing of heavy sleep, I finally began to speak on the subject Olga had patiently waited for me to bring up.

"As long as I'm around," I said, not taking my eyes off the highway which stretched ribbon-like through the uneventful West Texas landscape, "they're going to expect me to do everything. They'll never stop to consider that they have to assume some of the responsibility. What I've done is place them in a position where they'll either have to get busy and make up their minds to do something or else decide that the idea of busing their kids way the hell to Alpine isn't so bad a deal after all."

With that I fell quiet, contemplating the unresolved problem I had left behind. For several miles we rode in silence. Olga occasionally let her eyes stray from the road, stealing a quick glance at my tight-lipped profile. We were like parents who had finally come to grips with the fact that the time had come to let their child stand on its own two feet.

After a while she moved nearer to me and placed her head on my shoulder. "You're doing the right thing," she said in a voice hardly more than a whisper. "It will work out for the best."

But what if it doesn't? I asked myself. Here I am traveling halfway across the United States to spend the summer and I don't even know if I'm going to have a job when I get back. A man with any sense would stick around and look for another teaching job for September in case the bottom fell out of the situation in Terlingua.

At that particular moment I wondered briefly if my whole scheme wasn't born of insanity, the product of too many hours in the heat mending leaky pipes and patching holes in the roof. Too late now, I thought, what's done is done.

Glancing back at my still sleeping children, I smiled. "Why don't we stop up the way," I suggested, "and sneak in and have us a big glass of iced tea while the kids are sleeping?"

"Sounds good to me," Olga said.

Thus the subject was officially closed for the remainder of the trip. It had been years since we'd experienced the luxury of a vacation and we were going to make every effort to enjoy every minute of it.

Irene and Gus Rithianos were thrilled that we'd finally arrived. Irene had spent long hours in the kitchen preparing every imaginable dish that she felt her daughter and son-in-law might like and a variety of treats certain to satisfy the sweet tooth of her young granddaughters. The guest room was spotless, the sheets freshly changed and the coverlets on the beds turned back in neat, welcoming folds.

Gus, an outgoing man with a booming laugh, needed little time to charm Anna and Cassandra, and Irene could not even wait for Olga to unpack before seeking answers to the hundreds of questions she had stored up since last seeing her daughter.

It was a pleasurable several weeks for all of us. I often accompanied Gus down to the Greek restaurant he owned and operated, sampling the wares of the cooks and watching with admiration the confident, methodical manner in which he conducted his successful business. "It's a good business," Gus would often say as he surveyed the tables, making sure the linens and silverware were properly in place. "One of these days I'm going to get too tired to come down here every day, though. Maybe you would like to get into the business someday."

I would always smile at the transparent suggestion, the casual hint dropped in hopes that his son-in-law would consider settling down nearby so that Gus might enjoy his twilight years with his daughter close at hand and his precious grandchildren at his knee. "I'm afraid," I would say, "that I'm just a schoolteacher. All of this is way above my head." Each time Gus would laugh and drop the subject. He was aware of my dedication to teaching — how often Olga had written of it in her letters — and he did not intend to bring any kind of pressure or discomfort to our visit; he was simply glad to have us under his roof even for a while. He made it clear that his offer had an open end and let it go at that.

For us it was a rare chance to feel carefree. With handy grandparents eagerly volunteering to serve as baby-sitters, Olga and I took advantage of the freedom to see an occasional movie or go window-shopping at one of the huge, sprawling shopping centers nearby. We even made a short trip into New York City to sample the hustle and bustle of Manhattan, taking a carriage ride through Central Park and a walk down Fifth Avenue.

Aside from the brief report we had given Olga's parents about the situation at Terlingua shortly after our arrival, little was mentioned of the subject. Still, both of us would eagerly read the occasional letters that came from Donna Pepper and Daisy. There was seldom word of any progress or lack of same regarding the school board's preparation for the confrontation with the Texas Education Agency board, but we enjoyed hearing all the news from home; it provided a link with the reality we knew awaited when the vacation was over. The letters were usually chatty, telling of hot weather and the comings and goings of the townspeople, and always ended with a question about when the Joneses were going to return and suffer the 120-degree heat along with the rest of the natives.

The only sad note came the week before we were to begin the return trip to Texas: Phyllis Burton, wife of Brother Bob, had died after having been seriously ill for some time. Olga read the letter slowly and handed it to me. "I wish," she said, "we were there so we could attend the funeral."

There is nothing like a tragedy back home to set the pangs of homesickness to throbbing. Even before the disconcerting news, however, Olga and I had agreed it was getting time to begin our journey home. Pepper had phoned to say that the hearing date had been scheduled for the first Monday in August. He said he and Ben Simmons would arrive in Austin on Sunday and asked if I could be there to meet with them before they went before the board. "I think maybe we've got it worked out,"

Pepper had said over the poor connection. "I'll tell you about it when we see you in Austin. Tell Olga and the kids hello for us." I was eager to learn more, to know just how the confident sounding school board member had it "worked out," but I yielded to the crackling connection.

It was conceivable that the problems with the school accreditation might be worked out. The city of Terlingua might even possibly make a comeback someday. Who knew? Richard Nixon might even resurface as a public figure in days to come. Just about anything was possible except, it would seem, satisfactory telephone service in Brewster County, Texas.

Placing the receiver back in its cradle, I pulled a small plastic calendar from my wallet. Studying it, I determined that there would be time for a stopover in Corpus Christi for a few days before the trip to Austin. Olga and the children could wait at my parents' home while I attended the hearing. Besides, I wanted to have a talk with my father before meeting Ben and Pepper. Surely our appearance before this group of six Texas Education Agency officials, whose task it would be to determine life or death for the Terlingua School, could be little different from facing a trial jury. The advice of a good lawyer, I surmised, might come in handy.

My father, once openly disappointed by my decision to give up law studies and privately skeptical about my original decision to move to Terlingua, had in recent years looked upon my vocation with warming pride. He'd even taken to referring to me as "my boy, the teacher in Terlingua," in conversations over coffee in the courthouse cafeteria. Though he'd retired by now, Luther Jones had of late been seen regularly in the corridors of the courthouse, his almost daily appearances prompting several of his friends to ask if he had grown weary of the luxury of sleeping late. The purpose of his travels downtown, however, was to seek out attorneys with any knowledge of such things as public school education and accreditation. He studied law books with a fervor he had not experienced since his pre-bar exam days, hoping to find some obscure statute that might benefit our cause. By phone he urged my brother in the legislature, Luther, Jr., to have friends in Austin ask around to see what they might be able to find out about the Texas Education Agency's attitude toward the Terlingua School.

"The main problem you're facing," he told me as we sat in the living room the night after Olga and I arrived, "is finding someone who will carry out the responsibilities of superintendent in a businesslike manner, someone who will file the budgets and reports and matters of that nature on time."

I was quite aware of the situation. I had, in fact, told my father on previous occasions of the numerous problems I had faced as a result of Sam Thomas's tardiness in filling out forms and meeting TEA deadlines on crucial matters.

"We all know that," I answered. "You, me, the school board — and even ol' Sam, I'm sure. But what can we do? You can't go out and hire just anybody to assume his duties, and goodness knows we aren't exactly crawling with superintendent types out in my part of the country."

Dad nodded. "You and your school board have made it clear that you want to operate separately and apart from the Alpine School District," he observed, "and I agree with that.

But have you considered this? The superintendent of the

Alpine schools is qualified to handle the job you need to have shifted out of Judge Thomas's hands, right?"

I nodded.

"Why, then, couldn't he be paid by the Terlingua School to handle your paper work, be your superintendent at the same time he serves the Alpine schools? I don't think there would be any objection from his school board or from the people in Austin since his responsibilities to you wouldn't be that much, really, and could easily be handled in his spare time. I had a friend of mine do a little checking and it is all perfectly legal, though it isn't done very often. It would just be a matter of talking the fella in Alpine into doing it and then getting the go-ahead from his superiors."

I pondered the suggestion. Like most my father had been making to me since childhood, it made sense. Certainly it was worth a try, particularly in view of the fact that, unless Pepper had come up with one I was unaware of, there was no other idea to consider. I told Dad I would suggest it to the school board when we met the following Sunday in Austin.

"If you don't mind," he said, "I'd like to go with you." "Be glad to have you," I smiled. "The more the merrier."

Two days before the scheduled rendezvous in the state capital, I awoke with a fever and pain that I felt certain was going to tear the top of my head off. It sent me hurrying off to the nearest dentist in desperate search of relief from the agony.

By the time I got back I'd had two abscessed teeth pulled and was so pale and lethargic from the medication the dentist had administered that Olga immediately rushed me off to bed. With a case to plead, a cause to speak my piece on, I would arrive in Austin with my jaw so badly swollen that my words came out like those of a man with a rubber ball for a tongue.

My incapacity, however, turned out to be no problem since Glenn Pepper, having abandoned his work jeans and jacket for a business suit, had prepared, in a manner, a speech that was to gain even the admiration of my lawyer father. Sitting in the motel on the eve of the hearing, he rehearsed the points he hoped to make at the hearing. He carried with him letters of testimony from members of the community which spoke of the need for a school, the benefits that had been gained from the one they now had, and the commitments they were prepared to make to keep it in operation. Without exception the letters contained praise for my work, too.

Pepper, accompanied by Ben Simmons, made no attempt to hide his confidence. "Trent, folks back home are finally up on their hind legs about this thing. They're ready to do whatever is necessary. About a half-dozen came by and asked me if it would help if they came down to the hearing and put their two cents in. I'd hate to be the fella who turned us down, I'll tell you that for damn sure."

I smiled a lopsided half-smile, the best I could manage with my swollen jaw.

"The way I see it," Ben added, "all we've got to do is convince these fellas that our teacher here didn't go out last night and try to clean out some beer joint and get his face busted up in the process."

Dad's suggestion that Elmer Grounds, superintendent at Alpine, be offered the job of serving in that capacity for Terlingua seemed to be the last piece in the puzzle Glenn Pepper had obviously been working long and hard on.

"I feel sure," he said after hearing the proposal, "that we can work something out. I've had a number of talks with him about our situation and he's always lent a sympathetic ear. Fact is, he's offered to do anything he can to help."

"But how do we tell Sam?" I mumbled.

"A couple of weeks ago," Pepper said, "I finally made up my mind to drive over and have it out with Sam. I told him that I strongly felt we wouldn't be in this mess if he had just taken time to handle our business like he was supposed to, and that the only way we had a chance in hell of getting things straightened out was for him to agree to let somebody else handle the job. He just sat there and looked at me for a minute, kinda sadlike, and then you know what he said? He said, 'Glenn, you're a hundred percent right.' He said we should have had this talk a long time ago, that the job was just more than he could handle. He wasn't mad. Even said he would help find somebody to replace himself if we wanted him to."

I was relieved to know that the air had finally been cleared with Sam Thomas. While the middle-aged judge had caused me continued anger and frustration in years past, I couldn't help but like him. I had hoped the problem could be resolved with a minimum of ill will, and evidently Pepper had accomplished that.

The only hurdle that remained was the panel of six men who would stand in judgment of all our efforts the following morning.

Pepper, serving as spokesman, was nothing short of eloquent in his presentation; his painstaking preparation was further accented by his obvious sincerity. He spoke of his own family situation, of the hard work that had gone into carving a life from the desert country, of the benefits his children, particularly David, had realized from their attendance at the Terlingua School. He spoke in such glowing terms of my teaching ability and enthusiasm that I was concerned that my friend might be overdoing it a bit.

Evidently, however, the members of the panel didn't share my concern. Thus, on that first week of August, just a month before the school year would begin, the Terlingua School was granted a one-year probationary accreditation, becoming the only accredited one-teacher school in Texas. In the upcoming year it would have to meet some additional standards, which would then have to be ruled on by Phillips's office. But, compared to the demands we had already met, they seemed minor.

"The county board has to okay the Alpine superintendent's taking over for Judge Thomas," Phillips said at the close of the hearing, "but I see no real difficulty there. And since the new tax structure goes into effect at the first of the year, the school can borrow ahead on its tax revenue and get off to a proper start."

Later, as Pepper and I sat in Mr. Phillips's office, relaxing after the ordeal we had just gone through, the man who had officially given new life to the Terlingua School smiled and offered his congratulations.

"You know," said Phillips, a tired-looking man of middle

age who had no doubt sat in on more accreditation hearings than he could probably even begin to remember, "I went to an eight-grade school myself up in Grayson County – and it wasn't half-bad. In fact, I still have fond memories of those days. But let's face it, the one-teacher school is a dying thing, something for the history books. In the first place, it isn't all that practical in these days and times; and in the second place, there is no way one person can do the job that three or four can. And that's what you're asking one person to do when he assumes responsibility for teaching eight grades."

He then turned to Pepper, directing his conversation at him as if I weren't even in the room. "But Trent is bound and determined to make it work, isn't he? He's got more spunk than anyone I've run into in a long time. You can't help but admire him. I think if the truth were known he would probably have liked to be a missionary instead of a teacher.

Several years ago a gas company called me, looking for a teacher to go to North Africa and teach the kids of workers they had over there. I wish I had known Trent back then. Shoot, he'd have probably been on the next boat. But instead, Terlingua got him and I'd have to guess he's providing that community with the best educational program it's had since the mines closed down. Maybe even before.

"I think everyone on the panel was sympathetic to your cause. God, when you think about a bunch of little kids having to get up at something like four in the morning in the dead of winter to catch a school bus they're going to have to ride all the way across the county every day, you get to wondering if you would put your own kid through something like that.

"There wasn't a man in this office who wanted to close your little school down. We just had to wait, though, for you to come up with some solutions to your problems. That's the way we have to work here. When you were finally able to show how the tax rates were going to go up and provide needed financing and then offered a suggestion that the Alpine superintendent move in and lend a hand, that did it. That was what we needed to hear. Had to hear.

"I think you people are going to do all right." Indeed, I thought, we will.

And so the long battle was over. It was still hard to believe that we had finally won. Pepper and I eventually rose and thanked Mr. Phillips and escaped to the parking lot outside the modern red brick building which earlier in the day had looked so foreboding. Ben and my father were waiting for us.

"Well," said Pepper, smiling, "normally I hate to brag, but I think we did ourselves pretty proud in there."

"Mr. Pepper," said my father, "you did a helluva job. All of you did. You have every right to be proud." He placed his arm around me. "I guess it might be a good idea if you found a telephone and let mama and Olga know how things came out."

It was Olga who answered the call. "Honey," I said, "you better get busy packing things up. We've got to get home and start getting ready for the opening of school…"

She didn't hear anything else I said. Her scream of joy caused my mother to come running from another part of the house.

Mother's voice soon came on the phone. "Trent?" "It's me, Mom. What's the matter with Olga?" "She's crying, son. Is everything okay?"

"Mom," I said, "everything is fine. Just fine."

Afterword

The one room school house the Joneses operated out of in south Brewster County is still in use today and is the reading room for Terlingua Middle School. The new building they constructed became the library for many years and is also still is use. It is now the principal's office and the teacher workroom.

Until 1996, Terlingua schools only went through eighth grade. After eighth grade, students who attended high school had to be bused to Alpine, 80 miles from south county. Riding the school bus, they traveled 160 miles a day round trip and had to be ready to board the bus before daylight. Those who came from Lajitas, which is 17 miles from Terlingua, had another 34 mile round trip to travel to get to the bus stop. Each week the students were traveling almost 1,000 miles to get to high school.

The commute became known as "The Longest Ride" and was, at one time, thought to be the longest commute to school in the world.

In 1996, things improved for Terlingua students when the Terlingua Common School District began to offer high school classes in temporary buildings next to the old one room school and library. Much of the year, when the weather permitted (which is much of the year in the Big Bend), classes were held outside. But as the students sat in the shade of buildings and trees around the campus with a view of the Chisos Mountains and the vistas of the Big Bend, they watched something even more interesting begin to take shape on a patch of ground next to the old school—Big Bend High School.

A tenacious community fund raising effort raised the more than $600,000 needed to build the new school and in the fall of 1997 it opened.

Just before school started that first year, high school students showed up in August to help construction crews finish last minute details on the building. They were tired of riding that "yaller dog" to Alpine and were ready to go to school a little closer to home.

There were six students in Big Bend High's first graduating class in 1997. Only two in the class of 1998, the smallest class in the state of Texas that year. Subsequent graduating classes have averaged between ten and twenty per year. In recent years, the enrollment at Terlingua schools increased to an average of around 200 with about 60 in BBHS.

The high school was phase one of a three-part building plan. In 2002, phase two was implemented when another community fund drive generated enough money to build a new, modern library. It also serves as a community library, complete with terminals where the public can do research on the Internet and get e-mail.

Phase three will be an activities building which will include a cafetorium.

Extracurricular activities in Terlingua are a little different from most places. In the spring of 1998, BBHS started a golf team. Lajitas resort had a nine-hole course which was made available and both boys and girls golf teams were fielded.

In the fall of 1998, boys and girls cross-country and track teams were started and the first boys basketball team began play. Due to great distances in the Big Bend, BBHS athletic teams played or participated in only about a half dozen meets, games, or tournaments a year. In the case of the golf team, they were able to host a tournament. The boys basket-ball team played one home game per year—outdoors on a slab called the "Terlingua Dome." The rest of their games were on the road.

In the fall of 2001 girls and boys played together on the basketball team, playing only one home game a year and maybe five or six away from home and in 2002, the first girl's basketball team took the court.

One extracurricular area BBHS students have excelled in is University Interscholastic League competition. Both boys and girls have placed or won in district, regional, and state competitions in one act play, spelling and vocabulary, feature and editorial writing, literary and poetry criticism, and debate.

In 2004, twenty-six years after they left the Big Bend, Trent and Olga Jones returned for a visit and a reunion and were greeted by many of their students who came to reunite and reminisce about the great adventures they had in one of Texas' last one-room schoolhouses.

Trent and Olga Jones

When Trent and Olga Jones left Terlingua, they moved to Alpine, enrolled in Sul Ross State University, and obtained their masters degrees. They thought that with masters in hand they might seek more adventure in another remote place—Alaska. Instead, they settled in Boerne in the hill country of central Texas for a time, where Trent taught 7th and 8th grade and Olga started a career in real estate sales. When Olga began to do well selling real estate, Trent joined her in the business and the two made more in their first year than he had in two teaching school. In a short time they owned their home and three rental properties.

A few years later, they moved to Los Angeles. Their entree to California was a little rocky and the Jones were down to their last $500 before they sold their first property there but their fortunes took off after that first sale and since then both have enjoyed enviable success.

When their daughters graduated from college, Trent and Olga bought an RV and toured the back roads of America for two years. Anna has since become a Doctor of Physical Therapy (University of Southern California), and Cassandra has received a Masters of Fine Arts (Carnegie Mellon Institute in Pittsburgh).

Afterward they settled in Ojai, California where, according to Jones, they're surrounded by "blue skies, mountains, and the Los Padres National Forest." Being back in a small community was always their goal. In Ojai, Jones operates his own real estate company and Olga is a financial planner.

Carlton Stowers

Among the over two dozen books authored by Carlton Stowers are *TO THE LAST BREATH* and *CARELESS WHISPERS*, both winners of the Mystery Writers of America's Edgar Allen Poe Award as the Best Fact Crime Book of the Year, *SCREAM AT THE SKY, INNOCENCE LOST, OPEN SECRETS* and his autobiographical *SINS OF THE SON*.

Stowers' books have been selections of numerous book clubs, and five have been optioned by motion picture/TV productions companies. *CARELESS WHISPERS* inspired the CBS Movie of the Week, "Sworn to Vengeance," and *OPEN SECRETS* was the basis for the ABC miniseries, "Telling Secrets." *TO THE LAST BREATH* was included in *Readers' Digest's* prestigious Today's Best Non-Fiction anthology and his writings have been translated into German, French, Japanese, Swedish, Dutch, Afrikaans and Spanish.

Stowers has also authored a number of books on sports, ranging from *MARCUS*, the autobiography of NFL standout Marcus Allen, that spent six weeks on the *Los Angeles Times* bestseller list, to *DALLAS COWBOYS: THE FIRST 25 YEARS*, a history of the high profile organization which reached No. 1 on the *Dallas Morning News* bestseller list. An article he wrote on football in a small Texas town was selected for inclusion in the *2004 BEST AMERICAN SPORT WRITING* anthology.

As a collaborator, he has written books with western movie icons Roy Rogers and Dale Evans (*HAPPY TRAILS*), Olympic pole vaulter Billy Olsen (*REACHING HIGHER*), former

FBI Special Agent Larry Wansley (*FBI UNDERCOVER*), and private investigator William Dear (*PLEASE...DON'T KILL ME*). *WITHIN THESE WALLS*, written with former Texas prison chaplain Rev. Carroll Pickett, was the winner of the Writers' League of Texas' 2002 Violet Crown Award as the year's best book of Texas non-fiction and was a Critic's Choice of the *London Daily Mail*.

Stowers' *PARTNERS IN BLUE*, a 100-year history of the Dallas Police Department, received a citation from the Dallas Police Association. He has written two non-fiction children's books, *A HERO NAMED GEORGE* and *HARD LESSONS*, which have been used by numerous elementary schools in their anti-drug and anti-gang programs. His most recent children's book, *STRENGTH OF THE HEART*, was co-authored with Marcus Allen.

Stowers' articles have also appeared in such publications as *Sports Illustrated, TV Guide, Time, People, Parade, Good Housekeeping, Money, the New York Times*, and *Paris Match. DEATH IN A TEXAS DESERT*, a collection of crime stories he wrote for the alternative weekly, *Dallas Observer*, was published in 2003.

He has received numerous national and state awards for his journalism. A 16-time finalist in the annual five-state Dallas Press Club competition, he has won eight Katie Awards. He is a four time winner of the Stephen Philbin Award given by the Dallas Bar Association. In addition to the Edgar, *CARELESS WHISPERS* received the Oppie Award from the Southwestern Booksellers Association in the Reporting category. He was voted Dallas' Best Writer in a 1988 Dallas Observer poll and in 1997 was honored as Author of the Year by the Friends of the Duncanville Library. Most recently he earned a National Community Network Media Award for Exceptional Merit, was a finalist for the Eugene Pullian Journalism Writing Award, has twice received Lone Star Awards from the Houston Press Club, and was inducted into the Texas Institute of Letters.

CPSIA information can be obtained
at www.ICGtesting.com
Printed in the USA
LVHW012038111021
700151LV00014B/2003